Ku Klux Terror

Birmingham, Alabama
from 1866-Present

Michael Newton

4880 Lower Valley Road • Atglen, PA 19310

Dedication
For Mark Potok

Schiffer Books are available at special discounts for bulk purchases for sales promotions or premiums. Special editions, including personalized covers, corporate imprints, and excerpts can be created in large quantities for special needs. For more information contact the publisher:

Published by Schiffer Publishing, Ltd.
4880 Lower Valley Road
Atglen, PA 19310
Phone: (610) 593-1777; Fax: (610) 593-2002
E-mail: Info@schifferbooks.com

For the largest selection of fine reference books on this and related subjects, please visit our website at
www.schifferbooks.com
We are always looking for people to write books on new and related subjects.
If you have an idea for a book, please contact us at
proposals@schifferbooks.com

This book may be purchased from the publisher.
Please try your bookstore first.
You may write for a free catalog.

In Europe, Schiffer books are distributed by
Bushwood Books
6 Marksbury Ave.
Kew Gardens
Surrey TW9 4JF England
Phone: 44 (0) 20 8392 8585; Fax: 44 (0) 20 8392 9876
E-mail: info@bushwoodbooks.co.uk
Website: www.bushwoodbooks.co.uk

Other Schiffer Books By The Author:

Strange Kentucky Monsters
ISBN: 978-0-7643-3440-5 $14.99

Strange California Monsters
ISBN: 978-0-7643-3336-1 $14.99

Strange Indiana Monsters
ISBN: 0-7643-2608-2 $12.95

Strange Monsters of the Pacific Northwest
ISBN: 978-0-7643-3622-5 $16.99

Strange Pennsylvania Monsters
ISBN: 978-0-7643-3985-1 $19.99

Text by Michael Newton
Photos compiled by Michael Newton,
copyrighted as noted in text

Copyright © 2013 by Michael Newton
Library of Congress Control Number: 2013931304

Designed by Mark David Bowyer
Type set in Aachen BT / NewBaskerville BT

ISBN: 978-0-7643-4364-3
Printed in the United States of America

Contents

Acknowledgments

Thanks to David Frasier, friend, fellow author, and researcher *par excellence* at Indiana University's Lilly Library, for his invaluable contributions toward the completion of this book.

TENNESSEE TO THE NORTH

MISSISSIPPI TO THE WEST

GEORGIA TO THE EAST

FLORIDA TO THE SOUTH

OCEAN

LAUDERDALE
LIMESTONE
MADISON
JACKSON
COLBERT
FRANKLIN
LAWRENCE
MORGAN
MARSHALL
DEKALB
MARION
WINSTON
CULLMAN
CHEROKEE
ETOWAH
BLOUNT
LAMAR
FAYETTE
WALKER
ST. CLAIR
CALHOUN
JEFFERSON
CLEBURNE
Birmingham
PICKENS
TUSCALOOSA
SHELBY
TALLADEGA
CLAY
RANDOLPH
BIBB
COOSA
TALLAPOOSA
CHAMBERS
GREENE
CHILTON
HALE
PERRY
ELMORE
LEE
SUMTER
AUTAUGA
MACON
RUSSELL
MARENGO
DALLAS
Montgomery
MONT-GOMERY
BULLOCK
CHOCTAW
LOWNDES
WILCOX
BARBOUR
CLARKE
BUTLER
CRENSHAW
PIKE
MONROE
HENRY
WASHINGTON
CONECUH
COFFEE
DALE
COVINGTON
ESCAMBIA
GENEVA
HOUSTON
MOBILE
BALDWIN

Map of Alabama's counties.
Credit: U.S. Census Bureau

Preface

America's oldest terrorist organization began life as a rowdy social club. Some thirteen months after General Robert E. Lee surrendered to Ulysses Grant at Appomattox Court House in Virginia, six survivors of the Confederate army gathered in Pulaski, Tennessee, seeking a means of entertainment. Their chosen vehicle was a fraternal lodge, christened the Ku Klux Klan. They chose the first part of its name from *kuklos*—Greek for "circle," popularized by the antebellum Kuklos Adelphon college fraternity—and spelled "clan" with a *k* for uniformity.

In keeping with the tradition of secret brotherhoods, the founding officers chose cryptic titles for themselves: Grand Cyclops (president), Grand Magi (vice-president), Grand Turk (marshal), and Grand Exchequer (treasurer). The remaining pair were Lictors, guardians of the Klan's meeting place, called a "den." Each man designed his own peculiar costume and dragooned his wife or fiancée to fabricate it. Meeting after dark, they drank whisky and rode about on horses draped with sheets, amusing themselves with practical jokes.

A Reconstruction-era
Klan costume.
Credit: National Archives.

Given the time and place, it comes as no surprise that most of those crude jokes were played on African Americans, lately relieved from slavery and generally uneducated, since the South had banned instruction of its captive population under penalty of law. Likewise, since most young white men of the region were compelled to join in nightly slave patrols before the outbreak of the Civil War, they had been schooled in tactics of harassing blacks. It was a short step, then, to visiting black homes at night, dressed up as ghosts and demons, terrorizing former slaves and warning them against attempts to rise above "their place."

From there, the natural progression to a vigilante role was irresistible. Ex-slaves who violated tenets of the harsh "Black Codes," enacted by all former Rebel states in 1865, were frequently "corrected" by the ever-growing ranks of Klansmen who turned out by night to threaten, whip, and sometimes kill offenders.

Even then, the Klan might have been sidetracked and retired, if not for John Wilkes Booth. The gunshot that killed President Abraham Lincoln in April 1865 also doomed Presidential Reconstruction, tailored to reunify the nation "with malice toward none," once white voters in the former Confederate states renounced slavery and swore grudging loyalty to the Union. Successor Andrew Johnson sought to follow Lincoln's path, but he ran head-on into "radical" Republicans in Congress, outraged by the Black Codes and a spate of riots that left scores of freedmen dead.

Scrapping Lincoln's plan, Congress expelled the all-white legislators lately sent to Washington from Dixie and began erecting hurdles for readmission of the Rebel states. In addition to the Thirteenth Amendment abolishing slavery, each state would be required to ratify a Fourteenth (making freedmen citizens) and Fifteenth (granting them suffrage). The Black Codes were invalidated, and the South—except for Tennessee—was subdivided into military districts overseen by Union generals commanding 20,000 troops. In short, Dixie was occupied until such time as it saw fit to recognize "a perfect equality of the white and black races in every State of the Union."

In April 1867, three months before the federal Reconstruction Acts were passed over President Johnson's veto, Klansmen gathered in Nashville, Tennessee, to remodel their "hilarious social club" as an instrument of paramilitary resistance. They drafted a noble-sounding constitution, or "prescript," defining their purpose as protection of "the weak, the innocent, and the defenseless [i.e., southern whites] from the indignities, wrongs, and outrages of the lawless, the violent, and the brutal [blacks and Republicans]." The Klan vowed to "support the United States Constitution and constitutional laws"—which, as defined by Klansmen, ruled out any progress toward racial equality.

Klansmen raid a black home during Reconstruction.
Credit: Library of Congress

To carry out their lofty aims, Klan leaders divided the former Confederacy—dubbed an "Invisible Empire"—into realms (states), dominions (congressional districts), provinces (counties), and dens (local units). New ranks of officers were named, with a Grand Dragon and eight Hydras commanding each realm, a Grand Titan and six Furies supervising each dominion, a Grand Giant and four Goblins ruling each province, and a Grand Goblin commanding each den with various aides. Individual members were Ghouls. The "empire" at large would be ruled by a Grand Wizard and his ten Genii.

Selection of a Grand Wizard set the tone for all that followed. The Klansmen assembled in Nashville chose Nathan Bedford Forrest, an antebellum slave-trader and ruthless lieutenant general of Confederate cavalry during the Civil War. In addition to chronic insubordination, which included threatening the lives of his superiors in uniform, Forrest—still revered as a "hero" and "genius" in much of the South— was personally responsible for a massacre of Union troops at Fort Pillow, Tennessee, in April 1864. A Joint Committee on the Conduct of the War, convened by Congress shortly after Appomattox, concluded that most of the garrison's 297 dead—many of them African Americans—were murdered after they surrendered. While some Confederate apologists still reject that finding, author Richard Fuchs spoke for most historians in 2002, when he wrote:

> The affair at Fort Pillow was simply an orgy of death, a mass lynching to satisfy the basest of conduct—intentional murder—for the vilest of reasons—racism and personal enmity.

Forrest never publicly admitted joining the Klan, much less leading it. Questioned before Congress in 1871, he acknowledged joining a group whose members called themselves "Pale Faces," pled faulty memory on other points, dodged certain questions with refusal to incriminate himself, then claimed that there were 40,000 Klansmen in Tennessee alone, 550,000 throughout the South at large. Outside the hearing room, he smirked at a journalist's inquiry, telling the reporter, "I lied like a gentleman." On balance, as Stanley Horn admits, Forrest "was, beyond any reasonable doubt, the Grand Wizard of the Invisible Empire." His personal racism, casual acceptance of violence, and the impossibility of micro-managing a secret society active across thirteen states—including Kentucky and Missouri, which had not seceded from the Union—guaranteed the Klan's descent into rampant terrorism.

Alabama's first Klan dens were organized in late 1866 or early 1867, but violence did not erupt until March 1868, following a white boycott of February's election to approve a new state constitution. By then, another terrorist group—the Knights of the White Camellia, founded in Louisiana in May 1867—had arrived to compete with the Klan for members and public attention. Both groups staged parades, sent threatening notes to perceived enemies, and engaged in masked night-riding forays highlighted by flogging, arson, and murder.

Nathan Bedford Forrest, ""grand wizard" of the original KKK.
Credit: Library of Congress

Ryland Randolph of Tuscaloosa, publisher of the virulently racist *Independent Monitor,* soon became Alabama's most infamous Klansman, fighting public duels with his opponents (one of which cost him a leg), and vilifying "radicals" at the nearby state university. Despite his notoriety, however, he was not the Cotton State's grand dragon. Several sources, including a memoir published by one of the Klan's "immortal six" founders, name the state's first grand dragon as ex-Confederate general and lawyer James Holt Clanton of Montgomery. After September 27, 1871, when Clanton died in a duel with rival attorney David Nelson in Knoxville, Tennessee, he was reportedly succeeded as grand dragon by another ex-general, either William Henry Forney or John Tyler Morgan. Clanton and Forney both denied any ties to the Klan, but as Stanley Horn acknowledged, such denials were routine from Klansmen sworn to secrecy. Forney later served eight terms in the House of Representatives, while Morgan was elected six times to the U.S. Senate.

Whoever was in charge of Alabama's Klan, they did little or nothing to restrain local dens and their "ghouls." The state's most public Klansman, Ryland Randolph, was intemperance personified, and many other members followed his example. Homicides proliferated, often timed to coincide with state or federal elections, as the Klan worked overtime to "redeem" Alabama from "Radical Reconstruction." Whippings were routine, sometimes involving hundreds of lashes that left victims dying or crippled for life. Other targets were branded or castrated, and roving bands of Klansmen sometimes overcame their dread of "race-mixing" to rape black women. White victims were generally Republicans—dubbed "scalawags" if they were native-born, or "carpetbaggers" if they came to Alabama from the North. Primary targets were public officials, law enforcement officers who made an effort to restrain the Klan, and teachers assigned to lift freedmen from the state-enforced illiteracy of the antebellum era. Alabama's raiders also joined Klansmen in neighboring states for particular projects, including capture of black workers who fled from labor contracts amounting to virtual slavery, and for riots like the one that killed scores of victims in Meridian, Mississippi, in March 1871. The only defendant convicted in that case was an Alabamian charged with raping a black woman during the melee.

Finally, it was too much even for leading white-supremacists. On January 25, 1869, Wizard Forrest penned a letter curtailing Klan activity, commanding that disguises be "entirely abolished and destroyed" in the presence of each den's grand cyclops, further forbidding any public demonstrations without direct orders from a grand titan or some higher-ranking officer. While later touted as a general disbandment order, Forrest's letter actually ended with a statement that the Klan endured, more closely knit than ever, standing by for service in emergencies.

John Tyler Morgan, reputed "grand dragon" of Alabama's Klan.
Credit: Library of Congress

Whatever its intent, the order had no discernible impact outside of Tennessee and certain dens in northern Alabama. Ku Klux violence increased over the next two years in most of Alabama, Mississippi, Georgia, Florida, Kentucky, and the Carolinas, echoing in Washington, D.C., where Congress passed a new Enforcement Act on April 20, 1871. Commonly called the Ku Klux Act, that statute penalized conspirators who sought to subvert the government, intimidate witnesses or parties to legal action, threaten jurors, or travel in disguise to deprive others of rights guaranteed by the Fourteenth and Fifteenth Amendments. In worst-case scenarios, martial law could be declared—as President Grant did in South Carolina, later that year.

The net results were mixed, at best. In Alabama, by year's end, 130 Klansmen sat in jail, but none were brought to trial and many more escaped. A year later, throughout the South, federal prosecutors reported 325 cases disposed of, with 262 convictions. Most of those imprisoned served only a fraction of their sentences, and many pardons were dispensed during 1873, while charges for any crime other then murder were dropped. By then, it hardly mattered, since the Klan had done its work. Ex-Confederate Democrats regained control of Alabama's government in 1874, with the election of Governor George Smith Houston, and Dixie at large was "redeemed" for white-supremacist "home rule" two years later, when Republican presidential candidate Rutherford Hayes bargained with southern opponents, trading vital electoral votes for de facto federal abandonment of former slaves.

In spite of their brutality, Klansmen emerged from Reconstruction as heroes, honored and romanticized in print by novelists and scholars alike. They had fulfilled their purpose and ensured one-party rule in Dixie for the best part of a century to come. When they were needed by the all-white power structure, they would rise again.

President Rutherford Hayes "won" the election of 1876 through a bargain with southern leaders, including Klansmen.
Credit: Library of Congress

Chapter 1
The Magic City

Birmingham did not exist during the Alabama Klan's first reign of terror. Early settlers reached its future site in north-central Alabama by 1815, but poor soil barred the surrounding Jones Valley from contributing to the Cotton State's antebellum economy. What the area lacked in plantations, however, it more than made up for in mineral wealth, a fact recognized during Reconstruction by owners of the North and South Railroad (later the Louisville & Nashville line). With banker Josiah Morris of Montgomery, they formed the Elyton Land Company in December 1870, choosing James Powell as the firm's president a month later. Powell had recently returned from Britain and suggested naming Alabama's new industrial center after Birmingham, "the best workshop town in all England."

Birmingham, the "Magic City."
Credit: Library of Congress

Subsequently dubbed the "Duke of Birmingham," Powell began to blanket the state and nation with advertisements for lots in the "city of dreams" on June 1, 1871. Six months later, he had sold them all, and Birmingham received its municipal charter on December 19, 1871. Governor Robert Lindsay appointed Robert Henley as Birmingham's first mayor. James Powell succeeded Henley in 1873 and persuaded state lawmakers to let residents of surrounding Jefferson County select their own seat of government. Ironically, in light of subsequent events, ex-slaves empowered to vote by the Fifteenth Amendment tipped the scales for Birmingham, against competing Elyton.

Even then, Birmingham—later dubbed "The Magic City"—had to fight for its life. July of 1873 brought a deadly cholera epidemic, fled by thousands, while September witnessed the "Panic of 1873," a banking collapse in New York that cast America and Europe into six years of economic depression. The crash burst Birmingham's real estate bubble before any factories rose, and vanishing jobs drove more residents into exile.

Salvation came in the form of the Pratt Coal and Coke Company, owned by Truman Aldrich, James Sloss, and Henry DeBardeleben. Establishment of their Pratt Mines provided vital stimulus to Birmingham in 1878, followed by another boost when DeBardeleben and Thomas Hillman built the Alice Furnaces to mass-produce pig iron. James Sloss erected his City Furnaces in 1881, while Hillman brought his Tennessee Coal, Iron, and Steel Company (TCI) to Birmingham, buying up much of the property owned by DeBardeleben and Aldrich. Not to be outdone, DeBardeleben and William Underwood built the Mary Pratt Furnace (named for DeBardeleben's second daughter) in 1883. The Louisville & Nashville Railroad helped with cash investments and "special" freight rates, while Birmingham's pig iron production increased more than tenfold between 1880 and 1890. In 1907, U.S. Steel bought out TCI, and the Magic City's restoration was complete.

Bourbons

The growth of thriving industry in Birmingham was only one aspect of Alabama's economic recovery from the Civil War. The state still thrived on agriculture, ruled by planters of the Black Belt and Tennessee Valley, widely known as "Bourbons." While the roots of that term are obscure, it is traceable to the French House of Bourbon deposed by revolution in 1792, restored in 1814 with the abdication of Napoleon. Alabama's Bourbons were white-supremacist Democrats, hailed as "redeemers" of the state after 1874, who pledged to reverse all aspects of "radical" Reconstruction.

In broad strokes, whether they presided over factories or vast plantations, Bourbons craved low taxes, minimal state services, and cheap labor. Having restored control of Alabama by white, upper-class Democrats through fraud and terrorism, they sought to perpetuate that domination through similar methods, aided by the "Redeemer Constitution" of 1875. With the risk of federal intervention in mind, that document stopped short of disfranchising blacks, and in fact granted suffrage to "every male citizen of the United States" who had lived in Alabama for at least one year. In practice, though, black voters were manipulated and intimidated by the threat of violence or economic ruin via loss of jobs, unless they cast their ballots for the Democratic Party. Where all else failed, offending votes were "counted in and counted out"—a backroom tactic that involved recording Democratic ballots while ignoring others.

As it turned out, granting African Americans the right to vote served Bourbon interests in the 1890s and early 1900s, when the Populist Party campaigned against moneyed interests and sought to unite all workers regardless of race. Alabama Bourbons used the shibboleth of white supremacy to keep Caucasian voters in the Democratic column, while they used their standard tactics to ensure that blacks also voted against their own best interests. One historian remarked that "[f]raud had not been seen on such a scale since Reconstruction." Georgia's Thomas Edward Watson, twice defeated as the Populist presidential candidate in 1904 and 1908, grew so embittered that he spent the remainder of his life reviling blacks, Jews, and Catholics, promoting lynch mobs and revival of the Ku Klux Klan.

By the dawn of the twentieth century, Bourbons felt secure enough to air their racism in public. They convened a new constitutional convention in May 1901 and spent eighty-two days crafting a document designed to ensure white supremacy. Article VIII effectively disfranchised most black Alabamians by means of literacy tests, strict property qualifications, an annual poll tax, and a demand for proof of one year's steady employment. Whites who failed to measure up were rescued by a "grandfather clause" granting suffrage to any man who "understood" the U.S. Constitution (in a white registrar's opinion), and who was either a veteran of some nineteenth-century war or a veteran's descendant.

Violence remained a popular option whenever blacks "forgot their place" and offended hyper-sensitive whites. Police and county sheriffs were the first line of defense for white supremacy, with vigilantes ever ready to assist them. Alabama mobs lynched at least 276 victims between 1889 and 1918, with no tallies kept during the quarter-century immediately following the Civil War. All but thirty-two of those murdered were black, with ten of the slayings reported from Birmingham's Jefferson County. No statistics exist for African Americans killed by police or murdered in local encounters with white civilians.

Lynch mobs terrorized African Americans into subservience.
Credit: Library of Congress

Big Mules

While Democratic bosses finished the thirty-year task of undoing Reconstruction, Alabama industrialists strove to make Birmingham competitive with northern manufacturing centers. Daniel Pratt led the effort, purchasing Birmingham's Red Mountain Iron and Coal Company in 1872, installing son-in-law Henry DeBardeleben as manager. Six years later, as president, DeBardeleben renamed the firm Pratt Coal and Coke. In 1883, he built the Mary Pratt Furnace, named for his second daughter, pressing on to found the nearby town of Bessemer—eight miles west of Birmingham, founded by Henry DeBardeleben in 1886 and named for British engineer Henry Bessemer, inventor of the Bessemer process for mass-producing steel from molten pig iron—in 1887. Incorporated in 1889, Bessemer joined Birmingham as the twin colossi of Alabama's heavy industry.

Soon, the state's "big mules" of industry forged ties with large-scale planters of the Black Belt region—so called for its dark, rich soil, not racial population—who controlled the state legislature through the 1901 Constitution's apportionment formula. Both factions thrived on cheap labor and rock-bottom taxes, the former achieved by confining black workers to menial tasks and subverting organized labor through white fears of race-mixing social equality. Later, dread of communism would be added to the mix, but in the years before the Russian Revolution, racism alone sufficed.

Birmingham miners on strike in 1908.
Credit: Library of Congress

Birmingham mine workers.
Credit: Library of Congress

Still, some workers *did* organize, despite corporate propaganda, police harassment, and vigilante mayhem. District 20 of the United Mine Workers, created in 1898, struck against Birmingham facilities of U.S. Steel in July 1908, precipitating two months of heated rhetoric and sporadic violence. As one of the South's rare integrated unions, the

The workers' quarters.
Credit: Library of Congress

UMW epitomized white racist fears. Management hired scores of "gun thugs," replaced striking workers with black convicts "leased" from state prisons, and finally induced Governor Braxton Comer to declare martial law, patrolling the coal fields with state militia. Company goons snatched black UMW member William Millin from Brighton's jail and lynched him in August, prompting armed retaliation by the union. Governor Comer warned UMW leaders against nursing any fantasies of racial parity in Alabama, and on August 26, ended the strike by sending militiamen to raze the union's tent colonies.

The Klan Reborn

Southern historians—and some above the Mason-Dixon Line, as well—lionized Reconstruction-era Klansmen as the saviors and redeemers of endangered white civilization. The Klan's vicious crimes were either excused as legitimate self-defense against "radical" Republicans and rapacious blacks, or else blamed on the society's lapse into "low hands" during its final years. The same theme struck a chord in popular fiction, with Thomas Dixon, Jr. as its most renowned proponent.

A North Carolina native and son of a slave-owning Baptist minister, Dixon was born fifteen months before General Lee's surrender. One of his vivid childhood memories involved a Confederate widow's claim that a black man had raped her daughter. Klansmen hanged the alleged

Author Thomas Dixon, whose racist novels helped revive the KKK.
Credit: Library of Congress

offender in Shelby's town square and riddled his dangling body with bullets. With the smell of gun smoke in his nostrils, Dixon's mother told him that the vigilantes were "our people—they're guarding us from harm." Dixon's father and an uncle joined the KKK, with the uncle being named Chief of the Klan for Carolina's Piedmont region. Later, Dixon, Jr. attended Johns Hopkins University in Baltimore, befriending fellow student and future U.S. President Woodrow Wilson, but he left without graduating, to pursue a career on the stage.

Barred from stardom by his skeletal appearance—Dixon stood six-foot-three, but weighed only 150 pounds. He turned to politics and won election to North Carolina's General Assembly, although he had not yet attained voting age. In 1886, following his father's lead, Dixon was ordained as a Baptist minister, peddling his own brand of racist gospel from the Tarheel State to Boston and New York City. His great success, however, came through literature, specifically a trilogy of novels eulogizing slavery and the KKK: *The Leopard's Spots* (1902), *The Clansman* (1905), and *The Traitor* (1907). All were best-sellers, later adapted for the stage by Dixon, who cast himself in starring roles.

Movie director D.W. Griffith subsequently purchased rights to Dixon's work and, in 1915, combined them into America's first epic motion picture, titled *The Birth of a Nation*. A cinematic paean to a glorious Old South that never existed in fact, Griffith's film conformed to the prevailing view of heroic Klansmen pursuing black rapists and brigands (portrayed by white actors in blackface), and closed with a rhetorical title that asked, "Dare we dream of a golden day when the bestial War shall rule no more? But instead-the gentle Prince in the Hall of Brotherly Love in the City of Peace." Opposition to the film's racist theme was both immediate and emphatic, spearheaded by protests from the National Association for the Advancement of Colored People, founded in 1910.

Klansmen capture a black rapist (played by a white actor) in *The Birth of a Nation*. *Credit: National Archives*

Seeking public support, Dixon arranged a private White House screening for ex-classmate Woodrow Wilson, who reportedly observed, "It is like writing history with lightning, and my only regret is that it is all so terribly true." Further endorsement, later recanted, came from Chief Justice Edward White of the U.S. Supreme Court, a Louisiana native who acknowledged membership in the original Klan.

As *The Birth of a Nation* rolled on to record box-office profits, cries arose for a revival of the KKK. Dixon considered leading it himself, but demurred to continue his writing, publishing nineteen more novels before a stroke crippled him in 1939. Meanwhile, the work of resuscitating the Klan fell to William Joseph Simmons, an Alabama farmer's son and one-time Methodist minister (defrocked for "moral impairment"), who finally prospered as a recruiter for fraternal lodges. Simmons later claimed that while bedridden from a car accident, he experienced a vision of robed Klansmen galloping around his sickroom on horseback. While convalescing, he plagiarized and adapted the first Klan's prescript, inserting requirements that members be white Gentile Protestants, and fabricating a new lexicon of ranks and terms starting with the letters "kl." His brainchild would be called the Knights of the Ku Klux Klan, Inc.

With the framework on paper, Simmons timed his announcement of the Klan's rebirth to coincide with *The Birth of a Nation*'s premiere in Atlanta, Georgia. Bereft of members at the outset, he hired black men to pose in Klan robes for publicity photos, then set about recruiting followers from Atlanta's upper crust, the speaker of Georgia's state legislature among them. On Thanksgiving Eve he led his first recruits to the peak of Stone Mountain, outside Atlanta, and set fire to a cross whose light was visible throughout the city.

William Simmons (in skull mask) conducts a rally of the revived Ku Klux Klan. *Credit: National Archives*

Cross-burning, called "cross-lighting" since the latter 1970s by Klansmen seeking to reform their image, has its roots in Medieval Scotland. There, the fiery cross—or *Crann Tara*—served as a declaration of war between rival clans. Reconstruction-era Klansmen burned no crosses, but Thomas Dixon's novels imported the practice as a romantic touch, and William Simmons adopted the symbol as he had lifted so much of the earlier Klan's supposed philosophy. Today, the origins of cross-burning are largely forgotten outside of Scotland, while the flaming symbol is universally associated with racist harassment.

Despite the popularity of Dixon's novels and Griffith's epic film, encouraged by a wave of racism and nativism taking its cue from Georgia's Tom Watson and exacerbated by the First World War, the new Klan proved to be a slow starter. By 1919, after four years of recruiting, Simmons still claimed barely 2,000 dues-paying members. Most were Georgians, but the Klan had also planted "klaverns" (chapters) in Birmingham and Mobile, Alabama, during 1916.

Slim numbers notwithstanding, Alabama's Klansmen made their presence felt. Hooded members threatened shipyard strikers at Mobile in June 1918, beat one union organizer, and were prime suspects when the same man later vanished without a trace. During the same year, when steel workers struck in Birmingham, local Klansmen kidnapped their leader, as well. When not engaged in union-busting, robed knights spied on Jewish merchants, distributed anti-Catholic literature, and issued stern warnings to draft-dodgers.

Riding to Power

Despite the Klan's hectic and often violent activity, something was clearly missing. "Imperial Wizard" Simmons and his headquarters staff viewed the Klan as a cash cow, charging new recruits ten dollars per head, plus expenses for cheaply-made robes, other paraphernalia, and reams of literature—but to realize its full potential, they needed more members. Enter Edward Young Clarke and Elizabeth Tyler, sometime lovers and joint proprietors of the Southern Publicity Association. They huddled with Simmons, charted a campaign to hype the Klan nationwide, and hired hundreds of "kleagles" (recruiters) to canvass every state of the Union, emphasizing contact with veterans' groups and fraternal lodges. Starting in 1920, Clarke and Tyler brought the KKK nearly 100,000 members by summer 1921. At its peak of strength, in 1925, estimates of national Klan membership ranged from two to five million. A claim by the *Washington Post,* citing 8,904,887 members, was both impossibly precise and almost certainly exaggerated.

While Klan membership was technically restricted to white, native-born American Protestant men, Simmons and company missed no opportunity for profit. Soon, there were women's auxiliary units, separate youth corps for underage boys and girls—even an allied group for naturalized citizens, dubbed the Royal Riders of the Red Robe. Money poured into Atlanta, financing construction of an Imperial Headquarters, while Simmons reposed in a mansion called Klancrest. By 1922, the profits tempted greedy underlings to mount a palace coup against Simmons, deposing him in favor of rival Hiram Wesley Evans, another Alabama native lately employed as a dentist in Dallas, Texas.

Alabama soon emerged as one of the Klan's strongest realms, with estimates of total membership ranging from a conservative 50,000 to 115,910 (by the *Washington Post*). Grand Dragon James Esdale claimed 150,000 members in 1926, but statistics furnished by the Klan are notoriously inflated.

Hiram Evans (left) with a member of the original Reconstruction-era KKK.
Credit: Library of Congress

Whatever the exact number of Klansmen in Alabama, they were numerous enough to dominate local and state politics in the 1920s. Kluxer and millionaire coal operator Lycurgus Musgrove failed to unseat hostile incumbent U.S. Senator Oscar Underwood in 1920, but the Klan would scuttle Underwood's presidential hopes in 1924, and its strength persuaded him to decline a reelection bid in 1926. That same year saw klansman David Bibb Graves elected as governor, while knights of the Invisible Empire filled countless other state, county, and municipal offices. In Birmingham, estimates of Klan membership ranged from 14,000 to 18,000, more than half the city's total of registered voters. Klansman T.J. Shirley, Birmingham's police chief and later Jefferson County's sheriff, welcomed Ku Klux assistance on vice raids and advised other chiefs of police nationwide to do likewise. Historian William Snell asserts that most Birmingham police officers, "if not all of them," were Klansmen in the 1920s.

The KKK opposed Alabama Senator Oscar Underwood.
Credit: Library of Congress

The Alabama Klan's greatest political success story involved Birmingham attorney Hugo LaFayette Black. In August 1921, enraged by his daughter's conversion to Catholicism and her subsequent marriage to a Puerto Rican, Klansman and Methodist minister Edwin Stephenson murdered the priest who performed the wedding ceremony. At trial two months later, defense lawyer Black persuaded jurors to acquit his client on grounds of temporary insanity. That achievement, coupled with his own Klan membership, propelled Black into politics, replacing Oscar Underwood as one of Alabama's U.S. senators in 1927. (The other, James Thomas "Cotton Tom" Heflin, was also a Klansman.) Later, Black renounced the KKK, saying that he "would have joined any group if it helped get me votes," but his alliance with the Klan sparked controversy when President Franklin Roosevelt appointed Black to the U.S. Supreme Court in August 1937.

In 1924, the Klan played a pivotal role in the selection of a Democratic presidential candidate. Republican incumbent Calvin Coolidge maintained his reputation as "Silent Cal," refusing to mention the Klan or its attendant controversies. Democrats were divided on the issue when their national convention opened on June 24, at New York City's Madison Square Garden. A field of twenty-three contenders craved the Oval Office, and front-runner William Gibbs McAdoo—a native Tennessean, former Secretary of the Treasury—arrived with the Klan's endorsement in his pocket. While he did not praise the KKK, neither would he renounce it, prompting critics to brand him "Ku-Ku-McAdoo." His closest competition, Governor Alfred Smith, Jr. of New York, was doubly unacceptable to Klansmen as a Roman Catholic who favored ending Prohibition. Contender Oscar Underwood, already marked by Alabama Klansmen for removal from the Senate, still commanded the loyalty of his state's delegation, for whatever that was worth.

The convention soon degenerated into a wild free-for-all, with the KKK and Prohibition's failed "noble experiment" driving wedges into partisan fault lines. Amidst riotous debate, delegates cast 103 ballots before finally choosing a compromise candidate: former U.S. Solicitor General and Ambassador to Britain John William Davis, of West Virginia. Even then, it remained for them to argue out specific planks of the party's platform—including a demand by some to name the Klan as a divisive, un-American society. That push produced more screaming arguments, and several rounds of fisticuffs, before the anti-Klan plank was defeated by one-quarter of a vote. Instead, the party vaguely endorsed constitutional freedoms, while condemning "any effort to arouse religious or racial dissension." On election day, while the South cast its ballots en masse for Davis, Coolidge buried his opponent with a winning margin of 7.4 million votes.

Al Smith made another run for the White House in 1928, winning nomination on the convention's first ballot. Disgusted Klansmen then threw their support to Republican candidate Herbert Hoover, claiming victory when he defeated Smith by a margin of 6.3 million votes in November. Without question, anti-Catholic sentiment played a role in Smith's defeat, but the KKK was not its only purveyor, and Smith was equally reviled as a "wet" protégé of New York's corrupt Tammany Hall. A dubious Republican prosperity—already lost to Midwestern farmers, soon to be wiped out entirely by the Wall Street crash of 1929—likely secured as many votes for Hoover as all other issues put together. Urban Americans were living in the bubble of a dream about to burst. For most, the Klan was already a fading memory.

Presidential candidate Al Smith faced Klan opposition as a Catholic who opposed Prohibition. *Credit: Library of Congress*

White Terror

While the 1920s Klan had many faces—religious, fraternal, political, social—it made its most dramatic and violent impact as a vigilante movement. Where the original KKK had focused its mayhem on blacks and their white friends—"radical" Republicans, Union troops, northern "carpetbaggers" and southern-born "scalawags"—the new Klan's list of enemies included anyone who was not white, a native-born American, and Protestant. Some of the order's most violent rhetoric and outlandish conspiracy theories targeted Catholics, but there was animosity enough to go around. The list of "undesirables" included Jews, all immigrants except the "Aryans" of northwestern Europe, labor unions, bootleggers and dope peddlers, "radicals" and "Bolsheviks."

It should not be supposed that pale skin and attendance at the proper church were guarantees of safety from the Klan, however. Modern Klansmen, counseled and often led by ultra-conservative clergymen, threatened—and frequently whipped—white neighbors who offended Ku Klux sensibilities by idling, drinking, gambling, philandering, teenage "necking," neglecting spouses or children, keeping odd hours, or skipping church services. Criticizing the Klan was a major offense, and a fatal mistake in some cases. Even within the KKK itself, personality clashes could lead to arson and bloodshed. Alabama native George Thaxton Miller learned that lesson the hard way in 1927. A Klansman himself, and the confessed slayer of at least two black men, Miller ran afoul of the order when he objected to flogging of whites. For that, he was whipped himself, then subjected to a Klan boycott that closed his Crenshaw County sawmill and left him $95,000 in debt ($1.17 million today). Adding insult to injury, Miller also lost his black customers upon revealing his KKK membership.

Alabama was among the Klan's most violent realms during the twenties, though, as usual with the activities of secret groups, no reliable statistics are available for the number of victims threatened, assaulted, or murdered. In 1927, the *Birmingham News* ventured estimates that scores or hundreds had been flogged. The paper identified twelve white city residents whipped between May and September 1922, then lost track as the numbers began piling up. An outburst in March 1925, with twelve Birmingham raids in nine days, rebounded to damage the local Klan's political prospects. Judge Leon McCord branded Birmingham "the city of attacks," adding that local residents "have no one to blame but themselves." He singled out white jurors who acquitted floggers in the rare cases where they were charged, declaring that "the courts are no better than the juries that made them."

The Alabama Klan's worst year for violence was 1927. New state attorney general Charles McCall documented seventy floggings that summer, but the true number is anyone's guess. Victims were white and black, male and female, young and old. While many white Alabamians either applauded the crimes or declined to condemn them, opposition mounted from the *Birmingham News* and smaller local papers. The *Opp Weekly News* named the Klan as America's "greatest menace," while McCall—himself a member of the KKK who joined to gain political advantage—condemned Klansmen as "grotesque figures" and "human beasts." By year's end, even the staid Alabama Baptist Convention was moved to condemn floggers, admonishing all true Christians to do likewise.

Attorney General McCall soon resigned from the Klan and sought to prosecute hooded felons, but he found the path to trial obstructed by Governor Graves. Under fire by the *New York Times* as "the darling of the Klan," Graves ordered a survey of floggings, then refused to show McCall the final report. McCall obtained a copy by raiding a Ku Klux den, where he found the "classified" report among papers seized from "exalted cyclops" Frederick Thompson. Also in the file was a letter Grand Dragon James Esdale had written to Thompson, promising protection from Governor Graves, "which had been so nobly lent in the past." Unfazed by that embarrassment, Graves slashed state funding for Klan prosecutions to a miserly fifteen dollars per case. Most white juries still acquitted Klansmen, but McCall forged ahead for the remainder of his single term in office, sending a handful of offenders to prison.

Alabama Governor Bibb Graves, a KKK member, obstructed prosecution of Klan floggers.
Credit: Library of Congress

When not busy defending white supremacy or "Christian morals," Klansmen were pleased to serve Alabama's Big Mules as strikebreakers. During a 1920 coal strike, Klansmen launched a reign of terror against the miners, with cross-burnings, torchlight parades through mining camps, and subsequent beatings. Two years later, they whipped four striking railroad workers, plus one victim's daughter, who tried to defend him. Any miner or factory worker who supported unionization in Birmingham or Bessemer courted the Klan's attention, ranging from threats to flogging and murder. The mayhem went too far when it drove workers from the mines and mills entirely, prompting certain Big Mules to restrain their hooded lackeys, while the press weighed in more fervently against vigilantism. Grover Hall, editor of the *Montgomery Advertiser,* won a Pulitzer Prize for a four-month series of editorials blasting the Klan and Senator Tom Heflin.

Prosecution and withdrawal of Big Mule support hurt Alabama's Klan, without dissolving it. Historian Glenn Feldman pegs peak membership at 115,000 in 1925, declining to 94,301 in 1926, and 10,431 in 1927. The last two figures were suspiciously precise, but even with the swift decline, Feldman grants that the KKK "still had tremendous political strength in the state despite losses in the rank and file." Clearly, Grover Hall's contention that the Alabama Klan had been eradicated was wishful thinking at best, disingenuous posturing at worst.

Depression and Decline

The onset of the Great Depression after 1929 did more to hamper Alabama klannishness than any moral outrage over acts of violence. Historian David Chalmers estimates statewide membership at three thousand in 1929, further declining thereafter, and Tom Heflin lost his Senate seat to challenger John Bankhead II in 1930. Even so, the KKK would never die out altogether in the Cotton State. In fact, the lean years of the Thirties brought new causes to arouse surviving Klansmen and provoke sporadic bloodletting.

One such cause was the probably-false charge of rape filed against nine black youths at Scottsboro in March 1931. The accusers, two white girls of dubious reputation, inflamed racist sentiment against the defendants, aided by Klansmen who agitated in favor of lynching. Governor Benjamin Miller averted mass murder by mobilizing the National Guard, and the case proceeded to trial, with the defenders represented by attorneys from the Communist Party's International Labor Defense. After a convoluted series of trials, four defendants were exonerated, while the other five received sentences ranging from seventy-five years to death. Communist involvement in the case spurred Klan recruiting, seeming to prove the order's claim that only Reds concerned themselves with southern blacks.

Masked whippings continued sporadically throughout the 1930s, and Birmingham logged its first-known bombing in July 1931, at the height of a milk price war, while urban Klansmen focused on the threat of "radical" unionists. Two particular targets were the Alabama Sharecroppers Union, active from 1931 to 1936, and the larger Southern Tenant Farmers Union, organized in 1934. Both threatened to unite black and white sharecroppers against wealthy landlords, a menace that Klansmen—many impoverished white tenants among them—resisted in collaboration with local sheriffs and police. Mob violence was commonplace, claiming at least five lives. A Klansman in Luverne was also whipped and shot for warning black tenant farmers of impending Ku Klux raids.

Depression-era Birmingham harbored the Deep South headquarters of America's Communist Party, an ironic circumstance that galvanized police and Klansmen to aggressive action. A local coal strike in 1933 saw management mounting machine guns at several mines, and strike-related bombings rocked the city during February 1934. Strikers and "scabs" alike were killed before Bibb Graves—serving a second term as governor— deployed National Guardsmen, while federal agents investigated Red pamphleteering. Communist Party membership peaked in Birmingham that year, with one of a thousand local Reds, Joseph Gelders, tapped as leader and organizer for the party's International Labor Defense. Gelders himself came close to martyrdom in September 1936, when he

Hype vs. reality in 1930s Birmingham.
Credit: Library of Congress

was kidnapped and beaten by Birmingham Klansmen. A year later, the American Civil Liberties Union listed Birmingham as one of eleven "centers of repression" nationwide, where anti-communist violence was "continuous, not incidental," but the mayhem ceased overnight after U.S. Steel signed a union contract. That cessation, albeit temporary, seemed to ratify a claim that Klan raiding parties were directed "from tall buildings."

Conflict and Disbandment

Imperial Wizard Evans retired from the Klan in June 1939, passing control to James Colescott, an Indiana native, veterinarian, and former grand dragon of Ohio. Still declining in membership and prestige, the national Klan suffered further embarrassment in 1940, from its flirtation with the German-American Bund in New Jersey. Despite their anti-Semitism, southern knights generally disdained alliance with Nazis on the eve of America's entry into World War II, and Colescott felt compelled to dismiss the Garden State's grand dragon, Arthur Bell.

The Bund episode, coupled with a fresh spate of night-riding cases in Dixie, earned Colescott a summons from the House Committee on Un-American Activities in January 1942, but the wizard had little to fear from chairman Martin Dies or his Red-hunting colleagues. Dies scolded Colescott for the robed brotherhood's hatred of Catholics, noting the church's hard-line anti-communist stance, and urged a return "to the original objectives of the Klan." Committee member Joe Starnes, from Alabama, proved more amiable, declaring that "the Klan was just as American as the Baptist or Methodist Church, as the Lions Club or the Rotary Club." Queried by the press concerning more in-depth examination of the KKK, committee member John Rankin of Mississippi demurred, saying, "After all, the Ku Klux Klan is an American institution. Our job is to investigate foreign 'isms' and alien organizations."

Thus encouraged, Colescott went home to launch a new recruiting drive, but Pearl Harbor eclipsed home-front struggles, while draining the Klan's pool of potential able-bodied members into military service. Bigotry endured, of course, highlighted by five southern lynchings between January 1943 and August 1945. More lethal than any incident from Dixie was Detroit's three-day race riot of June 1943, wherein white mobs and police targeted African Americans, claiming thirty-four lives.

While individual Klansmen probably participated in those incidents, the national order confined itself to propaganda sorties during the war years. Repeated attacks on President Franklin Roosevelt's "Jew Deal" boomeranged against the Klan in April 1944, when the Bureau of Internal Revenue slapped Atlanta headquarters with a bill for $685,305 in delinquent taxes. Unable to pay the tab, Colescott convened a special "klonvokation" on April 23, which "repealed all decrees, vacated all officers, voided all charters, and relieved every Klansman of any obligation whatever." Colescott told reporters, "The Klan is dead—the whole thing is washed up. After Reconstruction when the Klan disbanded the Klansmen continued to function in clubs and on their own, and it will likely be that way from now on."

Or would it?

A few weeks later, speaking from retirement in Coral Gables, Florida, Colescott sang a different tune. "I am still Imperial Wizard," he declared. "The other officials still retain their titles, although of course the functions of us all are suspended." Wizard or not, Colescott vanished thereafter from the Klan and would not don a robe again before his death in January 1950. When Alabama's Klan resurfaced, it would pay no homage to Atlanta or to Colescott in the Sunshine State.

Joint meetings with the German-American Bund embarrassed Klansmen in 1940.
Credit: National Archives

Chapter 2
Bull's Law

Alabama left no stone unturned in pursuit of absolute apartheid. Miscegenation was declared a misdemeanor in 1867, upgraded to felony status in 1928. Segregated schools were mandated in 1875, reinforced by more statutes in 1878, 1901, and 1927. Railroad passenger cars were strictly segregated in 1891. Twenty years later, state lawmakers forbade any sheriff or jailer "to confine in the same room or apartment of any jail or prison white and Negro prisoners." In 1915, white female nurses were barred from treating black male patients. Public toilets fell under the "Jim Crow" rule in 1928. A rash of new laws passed in 1940 segregated waiting rooms at railroad stations, banned cohabitation by unmarried interracial couples, and eliminated integrated prison chain gangs. Bus station waiting rooms and ticket windows were segregated in 1945, as was seating aboard the buses.

Within that oppressive atmosphere, observers dubbed Birmingham America's "most-segregated" city—no small achievement in Dixie by the onset of the Great Depression. In Birmingham, city ordinances decreed that:

It shall be unlawful for any person in charge or control of any room, hall, theater, picture house, auditorium, yard, court, ballpark, public park, or other indoor or outdoor place, to which both white persons and Negroes are admitted, to cause, permit or allow herein or thereon any theatrical performance, picture exhibition, speech or educational or entertainment program of any kind whatsoever, unless such room, hall, theater, picture house, auditorium, yard, court, ball park, or other place, has entrances, exits, and seating or standing sections set aside for and assigned to the use of Negroes, unless the entrances, exits and seating or standing sections set aside for and assigned to the use of white persons are distinctly separated from those set aside for and assigned to the use of Negroes, by well defined physical barriers, and unless the members of each race are affectively restricted and confined to the sections set aside for and assigned to the use of such race.

A second ordinance covered dining:

It shall be unlawful to conduct a restaurant or other place of the serving of food in the city at which white and colored people are served in the same room, unless such white and colored persons are effectually separated by a solid partition extending from the floor upward to a distance of seven feet or higher, and unless a separate entrance from the street is provided for each compartment.

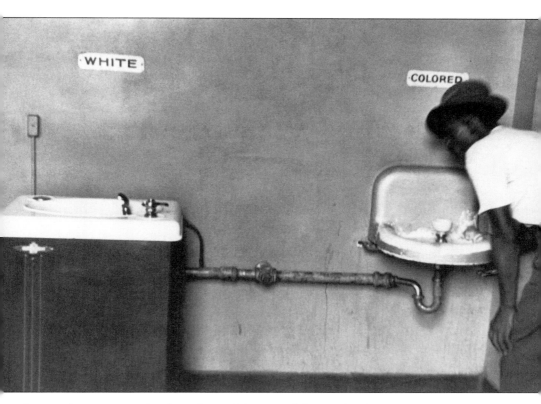

Segregation was pervasive throughout Alabama and the South at large.
Credit: Library of Congress

Yet another statute slammed the door on interracial recreation, stating:

> It shall be unlawful for a Negro and a white person to play together or in company with each other in any game of cards, dice, dominoes or checkers. Any person, who being the owner, proprietor or keeper or superintendent, of any tavern, inn, restaurant, or other public house or public place, or the clerk, servant or employee or such owner, proprietor, keeper or superintendent, knowingly permits a Negro and a white person to play together or in company with each other at any game with cards, dice, dominoes or checkers in his house or on his premises shall, on conviction, be punished as provided in Section 4.

And there were always loopholes to be closed, it seemed. Birmingham passed racial zoning laws in 1926, relegating black homes to former industrial districts. A 1930 ordinance required separate taxi cabs for black and white passengers. By then, each of Birmingham's courtrooms boasted two Bibles, ensuring that no white witness would risk contamination while swearing to tell the whole truth.

For nearly three decades, one man personified Birmingham's dogged devotion to segregation. From local celebrity status, he blossomed to become a national—then global—symbol of racist defiance, his very name synonymous with terrorism in the name of white supremacy.

The Bull

Theophilus Eugene Connor was born in Selma, Alabama, on July 11, 1897, the son of a railroad dispatcher named King Edward Connor. His mother died in 1905, whereupon King Edward moved the family to Atlanta, then dispersed his children to the homes of relatives.

Theophilus—reportedly named by his parents for a famous bandit—spent time in Birmingham and lost an eye there at an uncle's home when a playmate shot him with an air rifle. He also traveled widely with his father, later boasting of homes in thirty-six states, but the rootless lifestyle had consequences and he failed to graduate from high school.

In 1921, married and briefly settled in Dallas, Texas, Connor agreed to fill in for an ailing announcer at a local baseball park. The fans adored him, and it gave Connor ideas. In February 1922, he returned to Birmingham, calling baseball games for WKBC Radio. His colorful approach to sports casting, filling lulls in the action by "shooting the bull," soon earned Theophilus his lifelong sobriquet: Bull Connor.

Bull Connor (in hat) confers with Birmingham police officers.
Credit: Library of Congress

Next came a fling at politics. Encouraged by his fans, Connor ran for a seat in the Alabama House of Representatives in 1934, and surprised himself by winning the election. While serving in Montgomery, he befriended future governor James "Big Jim" Folsom, who "took Bull under his wing and advised him." Despite some suspiciously liberal behavior in the state legislature—Connor voted against a sedition bill aimed at suppressing labor unions—he still impressed Birmingham's elite with his local popularity. In 1937, a delegation of Big Mules encouraged Bull to seek election as the city's commissioner of public safety, a post that commanded the police and fire departments. Connor ran and won, pleasing white voters enough to win reelection handily in 1941, 1945, and 1949.

Above all else, Bull was a champion of white supremacy. And he was not alone.

Governor James "Big Jim" Folsom, a liberal by Alabama standards. *Credit: Library of Congress*

The Klan Revived Once More

As previously noted, James Colescott's ambiguous disbandment of the KKK in April 1944 applied only to the national order, known as the Knights of the Ku Klux Klan, Inc. Local units were free to proceed on their own initiative, and the earliest public announcement of a Ku Klux revival came from Atlanta on May 21, 1944, when Dr. Samuel Green obtained a charter for his Association of Georgia Klans. Six months later, a Ku Klux Klan of Florida announced its existence, with headquarters in Miami.

Dr. Samuel Green (holding sword) initiates new Klansmen in 1946.
Credit: National Archives

Alabama's Klan—reduced to an estimated 1,000 members in four shrunken klaverns—remained in the shadows until March 28, 1946, when eight crosses blazed overnight around Birmingham. On July 21, two local residents, Dr. E.P. Pruitt and roofing contractor William Hugh Morris, filed incorporation papers for their Federated Ku Klux Klans. Morris told reporters that the application "merely puts the Klan on a legal basis in Alabama; we have functioned as an independent unit for some good while. We have no connection with the old Klan, which has been defunct for some years, but our basic principles are the same: the protection of white womanhood and white supremacy. We have no animosity for the Negro and our organization is not based on hate, for any organization based on hate alone will fail. This revival is due to outside meddlers trying to cram social equality down our throats. All we want to do is keep the colored man in his place."

That would be no easy task with Harry Truman in the White House. Although himself a former Klansman and a lifelong racist—he referred to New York City as "Kiketown," described White House waiters as "an army of coons," and sent his fiancée a letter stating that: "I think one man is just as good as another so long as he's not a nigger or a Chinaman"— Truman issued executive orders desegregating America's armed forces and banning discrimination in hiring for federal jobs. Other "outside meddlers" included the NAACP, the Southern Negro Youth Conference, the United Mine Workers, and the Congress of Industrial Organizations (CIO), which pursued an ultimately futile "Operation Dixie" between 1946 and 1953, seeking in vain to unite southern workers regardless of race.

Bull Connor had set the tone for his whites-only administration on November 20, 1938, when the Southern Conference for Human Welfare held its inaugural meeting at Birmingham's Municipal Auditorium. Among the 1,500 delegates were First Lady Eleanor Roosevelt, Governor Bibb Graves, Alabama Senator Listor Hill, and Supreme Court Justice Hugo Black, gathered to discuss improvement of education, labor relations, and civil liberties in Dixie. Warned that roughly one-fourth of the SCHW delegates were African Americans, Connor arrived with his police, announcing that "Negroes and whites would not segregate together" as long as he was enforcing Birmingham's laws. That said, his men drove a peg into the auditorium's lawn, attached a ball of twine, and then unspooled it through the meeting hall, demanding that whites sit on one side, with blacks on the other. Only Mrs. Roosevelt defied him, dragging her chair into the middle of the aisle, and while Bull declined to arrest her, he had made his point.

Eight years later, with the Klan's revival underway, dispatches from the South were reminiscent of the 1920s. The U.S. Supreme Court banned segregation of interstate buses on June 3, 1946, but Alabama refused to comply. Governor Chauncey Sparks called the decision "fertilizer for the Ku Klux Klan," and whites in Athens, Alabama, rioted in protest on August 10. In Mobile, on November 18, Probate Judge Norvelle Leigh, Jr. granted a corporate charter to the Negro Voters and Veterans Association, despite a plea from William Morris and the Federated Klans that incorporation be denied "in the interest of continued white supremacy and common sense." Relative liberal James Folsom won election as governor that same month, but in March 1947, after controversial New Dealer Aubrey Williams predicted that the South would produce "the next great liberal movement in this country," letters postmarked from Montgomery threatened him with "a good working over" for criticizing the Klan.

The KKK's latest revival coincided with the onset of the Cold War and a Red scare unrivaled since 1919. A racist tabloid published in Birmingham, the *Southern Outlook*, self-described as the "Feature Newspaper of the American Way of Life," mixed strident anti-communism with the Klan's old brew of white supremacy, anti-Semitism, and union-bashing, spiced with racy photos and stories on par with those found in post-war "men's adventure" magazines. Klansman-publisher Horace Wilkinson hired Georgia kluxer "John Perkins" as his front man in Atlanta, unaware that Perkins—real name, Stetson Kennedy—had infiltrated the Klan on behalf of the New York-based Non-Sectarian Anti-Nazi League and would later air its secrets to the public nationwide.

Stetson Kennedy in Klan garb, with a pamphlet from The Columbians, Inc.
Credit: National Archives

Speaking of Nazis, the Klan had failed to learn its lesson after public friendship with the German-American Bund cost it thousands of members in 1940. America's first post-war fascist group—originally called The Columbian Workers Movement, then The Columbians Inc.—was founded in Atlanta by Birmingham native Emory Burke, on August 18, 1946. Its members wore familiar brown-shirted uniforms and sported a lightning bolt insignia borrowed from Adolf Hitler's SS, but they lacked *Der Führer*'s marginal finesse. Columbian membership applications asked new recruits only three simple questions: "Do you hate Negroes? Do you hate Jews? Do you have three dollars?" The Columbians logged their first arrests six weeks after going public, and several later wound up in prison on various charges before the group disbanded, but they would return to haunt the South a decade later, as the stronger and more violent National States Rights Party.

Meanwhile, Birmingham was facing turmoil of its own.

Dynamite Bob

Emory Overton Jackson was born in Georgia, but raised with his seven siblings in the black middle-class Birmingham enclave of Enon Ridge on the city's west side. He graduated from Atlanta's Morehouse College in 1932, then returned to Alabama as a schoolteacher, before joining the staff of the black *Birmingham World* in 1934. World War II interrupted his journalistic career, but Jackson was back in Birmingham by 1946, leading the NAACP's fight to overturn racist municipal zoning laws. His partner in that struggle was black attorney Arthur Davis Shores, a native of Jefferson County, born in September 1904.

Shores had graduated from Birmingham's Industrial High School in 1922 and earned a teaching degree from Talladega College in 1927, but he had to study law in Kansas and by correspondence, since the Cotton State barred African Americans from its state university. Shores passed Alabama's bar exam—then considered one of America's toughest—in 1937. He joined the NAACP, and before year's end successfully sued the Alabama Board of Registrars for its refusal to register seven black teachers as voters. In 1939, he persuaded jurors to convict a white policeman for assaulting a black labor leader. Three years later, Shores filed litigation that compelled the Jefferson County School Board to equalize pay for black and white teachers. In 1944, he persuaded the U.S. Supreme Court that the the Brotherhood of Locomotive Firemen and Enginemen should not exclude black members *and* bar blacks from railroad jobs on grounds that they had failed to join the union.

In 1946, Jackson and Shores joined NAACP attorney Thurgood Marshall in a legal challenge to Birmingham's municipal zoning law, which restricted black housing to areas formally zoned for commercial use. U.S. District Judge Clarence Mullin declared the 1926 ordinance unconstitutional on July 31 ,1947, thereby freeing African Americans to purchase homes in "border areas" formerly reserved for poor whites. Birmingham's top kleagle instantly branded that ruling an insult "to every white, Protestant, Gentile, Democrat in Alabama," and the KKK prepared for all-out war.

Sam Matthews, a black drill operator at one of Red Mountain's Ishkooda mines, was the first target, marked for purchasing a home in North Smithfield, on Birmingham's northwest side. Klansmen tried to warn Matthews off, painting a skull and crossbones on the house, then blasted it with dynamite on August 18, 1947, before Matthews and his family moved in. Bull Connor placed two detectives on the case "full-time," but they made no arrests.

While no two versions of what followed perfectly agree, all histories of Birmingham concur that numerous racial bombings continued thereafter, with estimates ranging from forty-five to "more than fifty" through autumn 1963. By 1949, the bitterly-contested Smithfield neighborhood was informally christened "Dynamite Hill," while local African Americans began to call the Magic City "Bombingham."

The Klan's point man in that bombing campaign was Robert Edward Chambliss, named for Confederate general Robert E. Lee, but known to his fellow knights as "Dynamite Bob." Born on January 14, 1904, in the industrial suburb of Pratt City, Chambliss learned demolition as a quarryman for Lone Star Cement and the Sloss pig-iron mines, married young to "some hellcat," and began his descent into alcoholism. In 1924, he and his father joined Birmingham's powerful Robert E. Lee klavern together. It was kismet for Bob. He had found his true calling.

Chambliss logged his first arrest in October 1935, for liquor violations. The following year, police charged him with deserting his wife and failing to support their children. Either case could have earned him a Ku Klux flogging, but his hooded brothers let Bob slide. When the national order dissolved in 1944, Chambliss was one of those who stuck around and subsequently joined the Federated Klans. Over the next two decades, he would pledge allegiance to one offshoot faction or another, always gravitating to the most extreme.

"Dynamite Bob" Chambliss
with his wife in 1947, the year
of his first bombings.
Credit: Library of Congress

Dixiecrats

President Truman's half-hearted campaign for black civil rights sparked a crisis for the Democratic Party in 1948. Republicans nominated New York Governor Thomas Dewey at their Philadelphia convention in June, but Democrats were bitterly divided when they gathered in the City of Brotherly Love on July 12. Northern liberals led by Minneapolis Mayor Hubert Humphrey pressed for a strong civil rights plank over dogged southern resistance. Bull Connor enlivened the proceedings, whooping through the aisles with a feathered headdress, demanding "civil rights for Indians," but his mood sobered when a majority passed the civil rights plank on July 13. Rising to speak for most of Alabama's delegates, he told the assembly:

> At this time, without fear but with disillusionment, we are carrying out our pledge to the people of Alabama. We bid you good-bye.

Cries of "good riddance" followed the defectors out of Constitution Hall and into a driving rainstorm.

Four days later, the splinter States' Rights Democratic Party—better known as "Dixiecrats"—rallied at Birmingham's Municipal Auditorium. Bull Connor welcomed the cheering delegates, then ceded the podium to Frank Dixon, a nephew of racist author Thomas Dixon and covert orchestrator of the Philadelphia walkout. Dixon blasted mainstream Democrats for trying "to reduce us to the status of a mongrel, inferior race, mixed in blood, our Anglo-Saxon heritage a mockery." Angry shouts of "No!" responded to his rhetorical question: "Do we belong in this kind of Democratic Party?" After Dixon declined nomination for president, the delegates required only one ballot to nominate South Carolina Governor Strom Thurmond in his place, with Mississippi Governor Fielding Wright as his running mate.

Southern journalists were not universally supportive of the new third party. The *Arkansas Gazette* branded the Dixiecrat movement "one of the most conspicuous failures in American political history." Closer to home, the *Montgomery Advertiser* condemned the Birmingham convention's "ugly carnival scene," while the *Anniston Star* chided Frank Dixon for sounding as if he were "addressing the Ku Klux Klan convocation."

Nor was the *Star* mistaken in that judgment. Black reporter Emory Jackson, seeking to cover the Dixiecrat convention for the *Birmingham World,* was ejected from the auditorium and told to run or risk a bullet. Welcome in the all-white crowd, meanwhile, were professional haters including:

Horace Wilkinson, a Birmingham Klansman in the 1920s, former judge, and defense attorney for indicted knights, producer of anti-Catholic fliers during the 1928 presidential election, who told reporters in 1948, "I'm against Truman for the same reason I was against Al Smith. He thinks too damn much of the nigger."

Gerald Lyman Kenneth Smith, a veteran of the 1930s pro-Nazi Silver Shirt Legion, former advisor to Louisiana "Kingfish" Huey Long, and an anti-Semitic clergyman, lately founder and chief of the Klan-friendly Christian Nationalist Crusade. Charged with sedition in 1944, Smith escaped conviction when the judge's death produced a mistrial and prosecutors dropped the case. While Strom Thurmond publicly disavowed Smith's support, Smith told reporters, "I was invited to the conference by one of the three heaviest financial supporters. I was invited to speak by some of the very individuals who effected Thurmond's nomination."

William Henry Davis "Alfalfa Bill" Murray, elderly ex-governor of Oklahoma, born in 1869, reduced by 1948 to authorship of pseudo-scientific tracts such as *The Negroes' Place in Call of Race,* charting ephemeral Jewish plots to corrupt the white race.

Jesse Benjamin Stoner, Georgia-born and lamed by polio as a toddler, late of Chattanooga, Tennessee, where he had joined Samuel Green's Association of Georgia Klans as a kleagle. During World War II, he penned a note to Congress, pleading for a resolution stating that "Jews are the children of the Devil." Dr. Green expelled him from the AGK after a wild speech in Atlanta, wherein Stoner roared, "I think we ought to kill all Jews just to save their unborn generations from going to Hell!" Undaunted by his ouster from the Klan, Stoner organized a Christian Anti-Jewish Party, first of many hate groups he would lead in years to come.

Jesse Stoner (with microphone) addresses a Klan rally.
Credit: Florida State Archives

As if the Dixiecrat defection was not bad enough, left-wing Democrats bolted on July 23, gathering in Philadelphia to nominate former Vice President Henry Wallace as the standard bearer for a new Progressive Party. Progressives advocated full equality for African Americans, welcomed black singer-activist Paul Robeson as a party spokesman, and nominated Birmingham native Virginia Foster Durr as a Senate candidate in Virginia, but Wallace's running mate, Senator Glen Hearst Taylor of Iowa, received a rude reception in Durr's home town. Arriving to address the Southern Negro Youth Conference, despite threats of Klan machine-gunners on the prowl, Taylor found most of Bull Connor's police department on hand to enforce segregated seating. Officers arrested Taylor when he bypassed the meeting hall's "white" entrance, lodging him in the jail's drunk tank. Burglars took advantage of the sideshow to stage a major raid downtown, but Connor did not seem to mind. Gloating, he told *Time* magazine:

> There's not enough room in town for Bull and the Commies.

Nor was there room for the Southern Negro Youth Conference in Connor's Birmingham. In April 1948, Bull summoned SNYC Executive Secretary Louis Burnham to City Hall, chastising him for publication of a pamphlet that referred to "the injustices of Klansmen's law." Glaring at Burnham, Connor growled, "There's no Klan here, but there will be if you persist with this meeting." Days later, when the pastor of Birmingham's all-black Sixteenth Street Baptist Church offered to host the SNYC rally, Connor came calling—and contradicted his statement to Burnham. If the meeting proceeded, Bull cautioned, there was a "risk of damage to church property." In fact, he said, God would "strike the church down" through His agents on earth—members of the very KKK which Connor claimed did not exist.

Pundits predicted a thrashing for President Truman on election day, with his party divided—and the *Chicago Tribune* famously jumped the gun with a headline reading: "Dewey Defeats Truman"—but all were proved wrong in the end. Truman emerged victorious with 24.1 million votes to Dewey's 21.9 million, while Dixiecrats carried five southern states with 1.16 million ballots and the Progressives did nearly as well, with 1.15 million. The election could be seen as national renunciation of bigotry, but Klansmen predictably missed the message.

Riding High

No evidence supports claims made by William Morris during 1949, that his Federated Klans had 30,000 members—7,000 in Birmingham alone—but enough Klansmen had rallied in the Cotton State to cause persistent trouble. In February 1948, after the Non-Sectarian Anti-Nazi League asked Governor Folsom to revoke the Klan's charter, Morris fired off a telegram accusing the league of trying "to destroy the very American principles for which we and our sons fought." Three days later, robed Klansmen with their license plates concealed drove through Munford and Tuskeegee, pausing en route to burn crosses. In June 1948, more than a hundred masked raiders stormed a Girl Scout camp outside Bessemer, where white scoutmasters had instructed black children. Jefferson County's sheriff deemed the raid "a good thing" and made no arrests. Dr. Pruitt denied any "official" action by the Federated Klans, but also praised the action, saying, "If I saw a mad dog or a snake I would shoot it. And some people act like mad dogs and snakes."

Klan demonstrations and violence proliferated during 1949.
Credit: Florida State Archives

A year later, on June 16, 1949, the *New York Times* reported that Birmingham Klansmen had assaulted three white victims—one of them a woman—within a week's time. Navy veteran Billy Stovall was whipped for allegedly leaving his children unattended, a charge that both he and his neighbors denied. Furious protests from veterans' groups prompted the state senate to ban public wearing of masks on June 17, and the Alabama House of Representatives followed suit on June 22, exempting only children on Halloween and revelers at Mobile's yearly version of Mardi Gras. Without naming the Klan directly, Governor Folsom ordered Attorney General A.A. Carmichael to revoke the state charters of "certain hooded organizations, by whatever name, [that] have committed unlawful acts of violence and intimidation against citizens of this state."

Dr. Pruitt issued the usual rote denials of Klan involvement and offered a $500 reward for conviction of any floggers, telling reporters:

> We do not intend to dissolve the Klan even if our charter is revoked. We will continue to meet and we will obey all laws.

With that in mind, he conceded that Klansmen would "discard their visors" except during ritual initiations "and similar ceremonies."

William Morris balked at that, advising journalists that:

> Dr. Pruitt doesn't have authority to hand out such an order, and I doubt that such action will be taken. We have not done anything, and therefore we do not intend to surrender anything.

Pruitt fired back in print, declaring, "I am president of the Klan," but Governor Folsom trumped the KKK by signing the anti-mask bill into law on June 26. Disgruntled, Morris said, "We will raise our visors—that is, unless the law is declared unconstitutional."

It was not, and while U.S. Attorney General Tom Clark praised Alabama's latest move from Washington, Alabama journalists appeared before a House Judiciary subcommittee in the nation's capital, detailing their state's latest reign of terror. Refusing to endorse proposed federal civil rights legislation, Clancy Lake of the *Birmingham News* reported that state police had worked "almost without sleep for weeks" and had done "a darned good job" of collecting evidence against hooded floggers. *Birmingham Post* reporter Clarke Stallworth described his own beating, when he was caught observing a recent Klan rally. Paul Trawich, of Jasper's *Union News*, recounted Klan warnings to "write about tea parties but leave the other stuff alone," yet still urged Congress to "leave this situation for us to handle."

Witnesses Irene Burton and her daughter, Sally, regaled the committee with descriptions of their whippings at Dora, with four male victims, on June 3, 1949. Their offense, according to hooded Klansmen who prayed aloud between the floggings, was promiscuous "dating." Nightriders had also burned a cross at the home of a female taxi driver, in Sumiton, but she blamed business competitors and told congressmen:

> We are proud of the Klan. It is the only law in Walker County.

Jefferson County's grand jury took a different view when it met to review recent cases on July 1, 1949. Judge R.J. Wheeler charged the panel to "get to the bottom of riotous, venomous, and malicious acts" by nocturnal prowlers. William Morris appeared before the grand jury on July 7, and was quickly jailed for contempt by Judge Wheeler when he refused to produce his Klan's membership list. The grand jury adjourned on July 8, but Morris remained in custody for seventeen days, until he was granted release on $500 bond. Back again on August 2, still empty-handed, Morris told Judge Wheeler:

> I made every effort to recover [the list]. I made every effort to get a new one. It was impossible.

And back to jail he went, locked up until September 20, when Morris grudgingly recreated a membership list "from memory."

While Morris was incarcerated, with a new grand jury hearing pending, Dr. Pruitt resigned as president of the Federated Klans on July 21. With regret, the septuagenarian told reporters:

> I differ with some of the elements that have wormed their way into the Klan—men who used Klan robes to go out and whip people.

And indeed, the Klan's crimes seemed undeniable. On July 10, 1949, Jefferson County indicted seventeen Klansmen on forty-four charges: twenty-eight counts of "flogging while masked," eight counts of illegal boycotting, six counts of burglary, one count of "carnal knowledge" (sexual assault), and two unspecified misdemeanors. Three of the defendants were past or present lawmen: Flat Creek constable Henry Nelson, part-time Brookline policeman James Shaffer, and ex-deputy sheriff Coleman "Brownie" Lollar of Jefferson County. Another was Birmingham's Dynamite Bob. The panel was embarrassed on July 16, by revelations that one of its members was a Klansman and another was a convicted felon, but it forged ahead to assure more indictments on July 22, bringing the total number of defendants to twenty-one.

After all the commotion, however, Alabama's purge of the Klan came to nothing. Coleman Lollar was acquitted at trial in October 1949, despite eyewitness accounts of his crimes from a female flogging victim and three former Klansmen, plus a threatening letter that bore his home address. Adamsville bus driver A. Byrd Carradine *was* convicted after three victims named him as their attacker, resulting in a six-month sentence and $500 fine, but Robert Chambliss and his other codefendants never went to trial. The only persons yet convicted under Alabama's anti-mask law were three African American youths from Ozark, jailed in August 1949 for donning faux Klan garb to frighten local black girls out of dating white boyfriends.

Klans Galore

While the Federated Klans were under fire in Birmingham, competitors lined up to poach Morris's membership. Dr. Green's Association of Georgia Klans claimed outposts beyond the Peach State's borders, including active Alabama klaverns in Anniston, Ashland, Lineville, Pell City, Talladega, and Tarrant City. A heart attack killed Green in August 1949, whereupon Atlanta policeman Sam Roper assumed command of the AGK. His spokesman in Alabama was Reverend Alvin Horn of Talladega, a defector from the Federated Klans whom William Morris branded a traitor. Horn replied through the *Birmingham News,* calling Morris "a man without authority," declaring that he (Horn) had "no intention of appearing before a traitor to answer a charge of treason."

While that internecine feud dragged on, a more flamboyant Klan leader appeared in the person of "Doctor" William Lycurgus Spinks, an aging ex-clergyman, self-proclaimed "sexology" expert, and occasional pretender to fame as the "reincarnation of George Washington." In 1930, Spinks fled South Carolina to escape prosecution for embezzlement, landing in Mississippi, where governor-Klansman Theodore Bilbo blocked his extradition to the Palmetto State. In Mississippi, Spinks lost one gubernatorial race and two campaigns to become tax collector, then sued Governor Wright for $50,000 after Wright "threw a slanderous dagger into [his] back." Moving on to Alabama, Spinks convened a gathering of six splinter Klans in Montgomery, on August 23, 1949, emerging as "Imperial Emperor" of the newly-formed Knights of the Ku Klux Klan of America. Spinks immediately claimed 265,000 members, with that number growing daily.

Less than three weeks later, on September 9, Spinks appeared on *Meet the Press* before inquisitors Drew Pearson, Lawrence Spivak, Edward

Folliard of the *Washington Post,* and Mary Craig from the *Press-Herald* in Portland, Maine. Claiming to speak for "every Klansman in America," whether they knew it or not, Spinks said that "[a]ll the niggers down South know that the best friend they've got on earth is the Knights of the Ku Klux Klan." On the subject of violence Spinks lied outrageously, saying, "There has never been a Klan in this United States that ever endorsed flogging or in any way violating the law," then quickly hedged his bets, adding, "I would not say that no klansman has ever flogged anybody." When Spivak asked Spinks, as a clergyman, if he thought the cross should be burned or borne, Spinks replied, "Both," then asked, "How you going to *borne* a cross? Who ever heard of such a fool thing?" Faced with denials that he ever served as Mississippi's grand dragon, Spinks raged, "I don't care what they claim. They're just like you. They claim anything on earth that pays off politically and financially."

Overall, it was not the Klan's finest hour. Ridiculed by leaders of rival Klans, Spinks left Montgomery on March 25, 1950, relocating his headquarters in Jackson, Mississippi. Six months later, on September 17, he announced his resignation from the KKK. Trying to unite the movement's fractious splinters had become "a nightmare," he declared. "It was just another case of not being able to play ball because too many boys wanted to be pitchers."

While Spinks hogged headlines, William Morris tried a merger of his own. Speaking from Atlanta on November 22, 1949, Sam Roper told reporters that his AGK had forged "a working agreement" with Alabama's Federated Klans, which he hoped "eventually will lead to consolidation." That move cost Morris more members, as disgruntled knights left the fold to create a rival Klan with chapters in Bessemer and Tarrant City. Florida Klan leader Bill Hendrix also raided Morris's ranks in early 1950, luring recruits into his fledgling Knights of the White Camellia, masquerading on occasion as the "National Christian Church."

Bombs Away!

Bull Connor's police played no part in the 1949 flogging cases, since most of those raids were conducted outside city limits. After Birmingham's initial bombings, city leaders had retrenched to fight the overturning of their racist zoning laws, a drawn-out legal effort that continued until January 1951, when the U.S. Supreme Court refused to upset a lower court's ruling in *City of Birmingham v. Monk,* declaring racist zoning statutes unconstitutional. Predictably, however, that fight was not confined entirely to the courtroom.

Birmingham Klansmen may be forgiven for thinking they had a free hand in the city. Cooper Green, president of the city commission (equivalent to mayor), was himself a former knight from the 1920s, and Bull Connor encouraged the Klan by both words and actions. Bob Chambliss worked at the city garage, allegedly maintaining and repairing police cars, though Connor himself summarized the bomber's mechanical skill by saying, "He could about change a tire." Nonetheless, Chambliss scored consistent semiannual efficiency ratings of 93 and 94 percent, while volunteering for police patrols in Birmingham's black neighborhoods. "You-all might need me along," he told officers, "to kill a nigger."

In fact, police appeared to need no help in that regard. Between 1947 and mid-1951 white police killed fifty-two African Americans in Alabama, half of them within Birmingham's city limits and ten more in surrounding Jefferson County. Commission President Green's own wife testified against one white officer in 1951, on charges of beating a helpless black prisoner, although the cop in question and Chief Floyd Eddins both branded her a liar. "Liberal" columnist John Temple Graves II advised readers of the *Birmingham Age-Herald* that:

> We would do better...to consider where the blame lies, with the police or with our Negro population.

Former Klansman Horace Wilderson had no doubt, declaring that:

> There is no justification for continually harping on a police officer for... whipping a prisoner who deserves every lick he receives.

Birmingham's calm before the storm ended in spring of 1949. Ku Klux threats resumed against black residents of North Smithfield, and members of an all-white "citizens' committee" visited the city commission on March 22, warning that "someone was going to get hurt" if blacks kept moving into College Hills and Graymont. Bull Connor promised the worried property owners that segregated zoning would persist at any cost.

Two nights later, on March 24, bombers struck three adjacent homes in North Smithfield. Two were owned by S.L. Green, a bishop of the African Methodist Episcopal Church and chancellor of Daniel Payne College for Negroes in Birmingham's Woodlawn district. The third was owned by another African American, John Madison. Dynamite Bob was back in business.

Summer heated up when two more black clergymen, Rev. Milton Curry Jr. and Rev. E.B. DeYampert, bought homes on the 1100 block of Center Street North, in North Smithfield. Bull Connor visited Curry personally, warning that "there may be trouble" if he occupied the newly-purchased house, and came away boasting to cronies that the family had vacated "two minutes" after meeting him. Bull also called on the DeYamperts, telling them that while they had a legal right to *own* their house they had no right to live in it. Connor's police also harassed a third black home owner in North Smithfield, convincing him to move away.

Bull's victory was not longstanding, though. Encouraged by friends and the NAACP, both the Currys and DeYamperts moved into their houses after all. City building inspector H.E. Hapgood weighed in next, harassing both families with nuisance citations, but they stood firm. Next came Bob Chambliss, warning the Currys and DeYamperts of bombs to follow unless they fled. To emphasize his point, masked knights burned crosses in North Smithfield and anonymous callers snarled, "If you don't get out of there, nigger, we'll blow you out." The last warning came in the form of identical notes to both families, reading:

> We regret that you don't have any place to go. But we will give you a clue. If you do not move out, we will send you somewhere, heaven or hell. You have the opportunity of deciding which place it will be. But we are of the opinion as long as you continue to be the cause of trouble, it may not be heaven. You and everyone else knows you are stalling and are just making a test case of it. We will see that the test comes out right. The city can hardly afford a couple of cops to guard you always.

July began with another visit by the white citizens' committee to Birmingham's commissioners. This time, the group's spokesman warned that "somebody is liable to start blowing up houses out there again" if black residents did not vacate their homes. On July 28, 1949, bombers left three sticks of dynamite at Rev. Curry's home, but the fuse burned out before it could detonate. Dynamite Bob did better on August 12, when two explosions shattered windows at the Curry and DeYampert homes.

Repeated bombings challenged residential integration in Birmingham.
Credit: House Committee on Un-American Activities

Bull Connor added insult to injury, briefly jailing one of the ministers on an unsupportable charge that he set off the charges himself in a bid to aid "those subversives who created this situation."

Angry now, 2,000 black Birminghamians rallied at Smithfield Court on August 17, demanding an end to local terrorism. Chief Eddins was on hand with several of his officers, glowering as Emory Jackson pointed them out to the crowd, saying:

> Well, it looks like we have a little more protection tonight than we usually have. There have been six bombings and no arrests....Not only that, but they've arrested three spectators. That's because it's easier to arrest spectators than bombers.

Jackson also accused Bull Connor of conspiring with vigilantes, and the meeting closed with resolutions seeking federal litigation by the NAACP.

A.C. Maclin, president of Birmingham's NAACP chapter, next carried a desegregation petition bearing 10,000 signatures to the city commission—and received Bull Connor's predictable response. "Maclin," Connor fumed, "if there is any bloodshed you know whose hands it will be on. We'll uphold the traditions of the South whether you or the NAACP like it or not." When Maclin asked Connor if he expected black citizens "to abide by anything less that what the Supreme Court of the United States rules," Connor snapped back, "I don't care what you do." Connor closed the meeting with charges that Maclin, Emory Jackson, and other integrationists were communist agents.

To the press, Connor predicted "an era of riots and bloodshed" to come, warning that lawyer Arthur Shores and "other agitators know good and well that the white people are not going to stand for abolition of segregation. If the courts do knock out our segregation ordinance, there is going to be bloodshed and the blood is going to be on the hands of those persons who would not let us live in peace. Neither the Army nor the Navy will be able to prevent bloodshed if these barriers are shoved aside."

Undaunted, Shores filed a federal class action suit that autumn, in the name of resident Mary Monk, seeking repeal of Birmingham's racist zoning ordinance. City fathers hired ex-Klansman Horace Wilkinson—branded "the worst race-baiter we have in this section" by Thurgood Marshall—to plead their case. On December 12, Marshall and Wilkinson met in federal court, where Wilkinson claimed that "Negro shacks" endangered property values in Birmingham's white neighborhoods. Furthermore, said Wilkinson, there was a "clear and present danger" of mayhem if integration proceeded. "There would be bloodshed and tragedy," he predicted. "There are some things that go beyond the written law—things created by the people and the Lord." Judge Clarence Mullins disagreed, ruling the segregation ordinance unconstitutional. Wilkinson immediately filed an appeal with the Fifth U.S. Circuit Court of Appeals in New Orleans.

Meanwhile, the Klan apparently revived its bombing war in Birmingham. *Apparently,* because the circumstances of the next reported incident are vague and garbled in accounts describing it. Author William Nunnelly, in his biography of Bull Connor, says that Arthur Shores hired a white man to infiltrate Birmingham's Klan and was thus forewarned of an arson plot aimed at another black home sometime in "early 1950." According to Shores, armed blacks ambushed the nightriders, killing one Klansman and wounding another. Police officer Jack Warren confirmed an incident "at about the same time," wherein officers sent to investigate a house-bombing heard "twelve or fifteen gunfire shots" but could not peg their source. Shores told Nunnelly that "there was never any investigation" of the shooting, and "it was not reported to the press," but recalled that "there were no more bombings or burnings up there" for roughly six years.

That claim, at least, is demonstrably incorrect. On April 22, 1950, Klansmen placed their third bomb at Milton Curry's home, nearly demolishing the structure. Nine days later, another bomb damaged the North Smithfield home of a black dentist, Dr. Joel Boykin. Police found an unexploded device—described by the press as a crude homemade aerial bomb—in the woods near Wheeler Dam, outside of Birmingham on September 23, and sent it to the FBI for analysis. On December 20, 1950, hours after the Fifth U.S. Circuit Court of Appeals rejected Horace Wilkinson's appeal, bombers struck Mary Monk's home in Birmingham. In May 1951, Klansmen returned to Center Street, burning two black-owned homes that had previously suffered bomb damage.

Somewhere in the midst of that violence, police collared Dynamite Bob, but the circumstances of his arrest are as garbled as those surrounding the alleged 1950 shootout. Historian Glenn Feldman says Chambliss was jailed for cursing at a group of African Americans, but a relative asserts that Bob was "arrested for a house bombing in 1950." According to that source, Bull Connor barred his own detectives and state police from questioning Chambliss, releasing Bob within a few hours and listing him simply as a "material witness." Whatever the actual case, it was too much for Commission President Cooper Green, who fired Chambliss from his mechanic's job for "conduct unbecoming a city employee."

Seeing Red

While the struggle over integrated neighborhoods continued in and out of court, Bull Connor focused on another target of his hatred: communists. The Korean War's outbreak, on June 25, 1950, had echoes in Birmingham as Connor ordered his police to track down "every known" communist within city limits. On July 8, his men jailed two local Reds—state Communist Party chairman Sam Hall, Jr. and associate Paul Rosenbloom—on vagrancy charges. Both were quickly convicted and sentenced to six months in jail, but that result failed to satisfy Klansmen who burned a cross at Hall's home on July 15. A note left at the scene, signed by the Federated Klans, warned Hall that "there is no room in this country for rattlesnakes, mad dogs, or Communists."

Chief Eddins vowed to investigate that incident, telling reporters:

> We aren't going to have Klan visits or cross-burnings in Birmingham. They just can't operate here. That's all there is to it.

Clearly, his boss felt otherwise, and local knights would suffer no significant police restraint under Connor's regime. While Sam Hall cited his service in World War II, declaring that: "I have not returned to my home state of Alabama to be intimidated by these hooded Hitlerites," Birmingham's city commission outlawed the Communist Party on July 18, giving its members forty-eight hours to leave town or face arrest.

Birmingham's anti-Red furor struck during a gubernatorial election year, with Governor Folsom barred by the state's constitution from seeking a second consecutive term. Sitting out the race to run—and win—again in 1954, Big Jim watched a mixed bag of fifteen hopefuls vie for his place in the governor's mansion. The victor, largely forgotten today, was Seth Gordon Persons, previously named by Klansman-governor Bibb Graves to head the state's Rural Electrification Authority in 1935. No evidence exists linking Persons himself to the KKK; in fact, he campaigned on a platform of abolishing the poll tax and was viewed as a progressive—at least, by 1950 Alabama standards.

Easily the most peculiar candidate on tap that year was U.S. Senate hopeful John Geraerdt Crommelin, Jr., lately a rear admiral in the U.S. Navy, cashiered in May 1950 for leaking confidential papers to the press and claiming that America's armed forces suffered under "a Prussian General Staff system of the type employed by Hitler." If true, that should have pleased him, since Crommelin was also an outspoken white-supremacist and anti-Semite, seemingly incapable of facing any problem without blaming it on Jews. In years to come, he would attach himself to different Klan and neo-Nazi factions, but in 1950, Crommelin was on his own, distributing fliers that promised a vote for him would be a vote against the "Communist-Jewish Conspirators" scheming to "destroy Christianity...eliminate all racial distinctions except the so-called Jewish race, which will then become the master race with headquarters in Israel and the United Nations...and from these two communications centers, rule a slave-like world population of copper-colored human mongrels." Despite his extremism, or because of it, Crommelin persuaded 23.5 percent of Alabama's voters to mark their ballots in his favor.

The Klan Survives

Despite intermittent campaigns of what Glenn Feldman calls "soft resistance" by Alabama's power structure, including occasional knocks from the leading newspapers, Klansmen held their ground through the remainder of the early 1950s, waiting for another cause to boost their membership. Bob Chambliss might have complained that the KKK was "going soft," while the *Montgomery Advertiser* called its members "self-righteous, bigoted punks," but its klaverns persisted and sporadic violence continued.

In Chambers County, on the Georgia border, residents found an eight-year-old white girl, barefoot and barely dressed in frigid weather, weeping hysterically at her mother's grave. On learning that she had been beaten by her father and stepmother, Klansmen rallied to punish the couple, flogging both in retaliation. Local police, sharing a general opinion that the raid was justified, failed to investigate.

Next door, in Clay County, a gang of Lineville Klansmen kidnapped a black employee of the local Ford dealership, accused of letting his "wandering eyes" stray toward white women during his daily lunch breaks. Afterward, the local klavern's leader boasted that "one night they went and got that nigger. He was took out to one of the pulpwood roads and they gave him a lesson in some common ethics." Again, police did nothing.

In Jefferson County itself, Klansmen from Ensley—a Birmingham suburb—kidnapped a black teenager they suspected as a "peeping Tom," beat him, then took him to the home of a supposed white victim. When the woman told the raiders they had snatched the wrong boy, they released him without apologies. Witnesses gave police the license number of the floggers' car, but no investigation followed. When the teen's parents sought action, Ensley's finest brushed them off by saying "they were busy and it was late."

Some of the worst violence occurred in Talladega County and environs, home of Rev. Alvin Horn. The local prosecutor was a former 1920s Klansman who apparently saw little reason to investigate the order's crimes, which included the abduction of a Talladega café owner, snatched from the city's main street and whipped for hiring black employees. Horn himself posted a reward for capture and conviction of the floggers, but his money was safe. No arrests resulted.

Pell City, north of Talladega in St. Clair County, was a particular hotspot for Ku Klux action. Klansmen grabbed one white victim on Main Street, half a block from police headquarters, and drove him to some nearby woods, where he was whipped "for not working enough." On February 22, 1950, another band of raiders targeted a second "slacker"—Charlie Hurst, a white Pell City merchant who had recently retired due to a chronic lung disease. While dragging Hurst from his home to their car, the Klansmen were surprised by Hurst's son, armed with a rifle. Gunfire ensued, killing Hurst and wounding his son. Four days later,

Klansman Roy Heath, a Methodist preacher, confessed his role in the crime to his sons, claiming that Alvin Horn planned "to put it all on me." That said, Heath shot and killed himself.

At last, police were forced to act. They jailed Horn, Pell City exalted cyclops Louis Harrison, and five other knights—Charles Carlisle, ex-policeman C.M. Hunter, Claude Luker, Albert Wilson, and son Jesse Wilson—on charges of murder "with malice aforethought," a capital crime.

Rev. Alvin Horn, sometime grand dragon of the 1950s Alabama Klan.
Credit: Library of Congress

However, despite Heath's confession and various items of physical evidence, only Carlisle was convicted, on a reduced charge of manslaughter. He received a five-year sentence in June 1950, while jurors acquitted Horn and Luker. Prosecutors dropped Jesse Wilson's charges after a mistrial. Hunter and Albert Wilson never faced trial.

Exit the Bull

By 1951, Bull Connor seemed to fear no man. In June of that year, after Emory Jackson detailed cases of Birmingham police brutality before the NAACP's Atlanta convention, Connor dropped by to threaten him personally. Bull was the darling of white Birmingham, its stalwart defender, front man, and mouthpiece. While not a member of the Ku Klux Klan himself, by all accounts, he had the hooded legions at his beck and call.

Until the week before Christmas.

On December 21, 1951, Birmingham detective Henry Darnell entered the Tutwiler Hotel, the city's premier hostelry since 1914. Darnell later claimed that he had received an anonymous tip of a crime in progress: an unmarried couple had occupied Room 760 in violation of a city ordinance forbidding extramarital cohabitation. Darnell spent twenty minutes pounding on the door, and had begun dismantling its lock when Connor opened up at last. Behind him, fully dressed—including hat and overcoat—stood one Christina Brown, Bull's secretary, twenty years his junior.

Connor said their presence in the room was innocent, and warned Darnell that an arrest "will ruin me politically." Darnell consulted Captain C.E. Huey, then left without filing charges, but Connor tried to hedge his bets days later, sending Darnell a note that reiterated his innocence. Bull and Miss Darnell, the note explained, had only been "talking" for five minutes when Darnell arrived on the scene. Angry now, Darnell filed charges against both defendants on December 26, and the case went to trial before Judge Ralph Parker on January 4, 1952.

Testimony in the case revealed that Darnell disliked Connor and had planned to run against him in the next election. After the *Birmingham News* leaked Darnell's political plans, Bull had begun investigating him, including examination of Darnell's tax records. *Post-Herald* reporter Bill Mobley, present at the Tutwiler raid, testified under oath that Captain Huey had secured Bull's promise to stop harassing Darnell, in exchange for a pass on the morals charge. On January 6, Judge Parker convicted Connor on charges of disorderly conduct, extramarital sexual intercourse, and joint occupancy of a room with a member of the opposite sex. Bull received the maximum sentence—six months in jail and a $100 fine—but appealed the verdict to Alabama's Supreme Court, which overturned his conviction in August 1952, on grounds that Birmingham's laws were too vague.

Meanwhile, in February 1952, Bull's fellow commissioners appointed a citizen's committee to investigate allegations of corruption and disharmony within the Birmingham Police Department. That panel deemed Connor "deficient in executive ability," asserted that he "lacked an objective outlook," and charged that he "conducted himself in a frequently imperious manner." Committee member H.A. Berg privately added that Bull had "definitely destroyed his future usefulness as head of the Police Department."

A year later, on February 28, 1953, Connor spent thirty minutes on radio and television explaining his decision not to stand for reelection. While claiming falsely that he had "cleaned up crime" in Birmingham, he added, "I feel that, due to the strong feelings which have arisen in unparalleled attacks against me, I should step aside from public office and, by doing so, offer my contribution toward a continuance of law enforcement and law abiding record that we have now." The decision was "painful," he said, but "it is in the people's interest for me to take this step now."

Bull was out...at least, for the moment.

Chapter 3
Ace

By the time Bull Connor abandoned his seat on Birmingham's city council, segregated schools were under fire from an unexpected quarter. A Kansas statute passed in 1879 banned segregation in secondary education, but permitted local school districts to maintain separate facilities "below the high school level." Topeka's high school had been integrated from its start, in 1871, and middle schools had followed in 1941, but elementary schools remained segregated a decade later. In practice, that meant that Oliver Brown's daughter, Linda, had to walk past all-white Sumner Elementary, seven blocks from home, to catch a bus for all-black Monroe Elementary, one mile away. In 1951, the Browns and eleven other parents filed suit in federal court, on behalf of their twenty children, to desegregate Topeka's primary schools.

The district court ruled against them, citing a U.S. Supreme Court precedent from *Plessy v. Ferguson* (1896), officially approving "separate but equal" facilities. While conceding that segregation adversely affected minority students, the court found Topeka's separate schools to be "substantially equal" with respect to buildings, curricula, and qualification of teachers. The plaintiffs and their NAACP attorneys appealed that decision to the U.S. Supreme Court in Washington, D.C.

There, the nine justices combined *Brown v. Board of Education of Topeka* with five similar cases filed in Delaware, the District of Columbia, South Carolina and Virginia. Only one of the cases so far—*Gebhart v. Belton,* from Delaware—had produced a district court order to integrate white schools on grounds that black schools were physically inferior. The Supreme Court heard the *Brown* case in December 1952, but was unable to decide it and scheduled a rehearing in December 1953. At issue: a question as to whether the Fourteenth Amendment's "equal protection" clause forbade segregated education regardless of physical parity between schools.

Finally, on May 17, 1954, Chief Justice Earl Warren announced the court's unanimous decision. Segregated schools were "inherently unequal," since separation "has a detrimental effect upon the colored children. The impact is greater when it has the sanction of the law, for the policy of separating the races is usually interpreted as denoting the inferiority of the negro group. A sense of inferiority affects the motivation of a child to learn." States where segregation flourished were commanded to integrate their schools "with all deliberate speed."

Shock waves from that order spread through Dixie with the impact of a nuclear explosion.

Deliberate Speed

Brown galvanized the South, but any hope of sweeping change was swiftly dashed. By May 1962, only 0.1 percent of African American children in former Confederate states shared classes with whites. From that, observers calculated that full integration should be accomplished by 9256 C.E.—7,288 years in the future. Even that goal was unrealistic in Alabama, Mississippi, and South Carolina, where eight years of "deliberate speed" had failed to integrate a single school.

One baby-step had nearly been achieved in Birmingham, in January 1954, when city commissioners passed an ordinance permitting integrated baseball and football games. Hugh Locke—a Dixiecrat leader, 1920s Klansman, and suspected mastermind of bombings on Dynamite Hill—promptly formed a Citizens' Segregation Committee to repeal the law. Locke explained his fear:

> Allowing a few Negroes to play baseball here will wind up with Negroes and whites marrying. People are saying that all this has to come sometime, so let's get it over with now. We want to stop that.

His group obtained 5,000 petition signatures to force a referendum vote, and racism carried the day, ensuring for the moment that a home run would not find black players sliding into white bedrooms.

As for integrated schools in Birmingham, forget it. Commission president Jimmy Morgan declared himself "unalterably opposed" to the *Brown* decision, while local newspapers echoed the antebellum cry of "states' rights," raised most volubly whenever states are bent on doing someone wrong. The *Birmingham Post-Herald* voiced "deep regret" over the Warren Court's ruling, while the *News* took a sly turn, advising readers that while the judgment banned *segregation*, it did not technically require *integration*.

That kind of double-talk could only go so far toward preserving the hallowed "Southern way of life," however. James Folsom, elected to a second term as governor in 1954, was liberal by Alabama standards, but he could not dam the flood of racist legislation generated by state lawmakers in response to *Brown*. Bull Connor tried to stage a comeback that same year, opposing popular incumbent Holt McDowell to become sheriff of Jefferson County, but voters rebuffed him. Supporter James Simpson reminded Bull that his—Connor's—recent scandal "was, unfortunately, very present in the minds of everybody, I fear, during the campaign."

Birmingham's white electorate needed more time to forget—and to tremble in fear at the prospect of African American equality.

Councils and Klans

Brown warned "respectable" racists—the Big Mules, Bourbons, and others frequently described without a hint of irony as the South's "best people"—that only organized resistance would preserve Jim Crow. With Hugh Locke's example in mind, colleague Sidney Smyer founded a new American States Rights Association, advertising for members statewide. Similar groups sprang up across the South, including the Southern Gentlemen, White Brotherhood, Christian Civic League, Association of Catholic Laymen, even a National Association for the Advancement of White People. Still, for all their racist zeal, they lacked the will and wherewithal to forge a solid front for what southern spokesmen were already calling "massive resistance."

In July 1954, a group of wealthy segregationists met in Sunflower County, Mississippi, home of longtime U.S. Senator James Eastland. Together, they founded the first chapter of a new resistance movement, the Citizens' Council, pledged to preserve apartheid by all legal means. They shunned secrecy and disavowed any link to the "nefarious Ku Klux Klans," though membership would sometimes overlap between the groups and council members would be linked to terrorist actions in several states. Upstanding members of the new group even bridled at media references to "White Citizens' Councils," as if black members might be hiding somewhere, but in fact the movement *was* all white and pledged to white supremacy.

Ex-judge and Council spokesman Thomas Pickens Brady tried to set the standard for "legitimate" racism, announcing that he had twice rejected invitations to join the KKK "because they hid their faces and did things that you and I wouldn't approve of." Nonetheless, the Councils welcomed anti-Semites to their ranks, reprinting literature from Gerald L.K. Smith's Christian Nationalist Crusade, "Jayhawk Nazi" Gerald Winrod's defunct fascist tabloid *The Defender,* and other tainted sources. Even so, Florida Klansman Bill Hendrix found fault, declaring that council founder Robert Patterson "was dominated by the Jews and the Citizens' Councils are full of Jews."

Bull Connor addresses an Alabama Citizens' Council meeting.
Credit: Library of Congress

If so, they kept their heads down and the mostly-Christian movement spread like wildfire. Alabama's first recognized Citizens' Councils surfaced in October 1955, two months after black petitioners asked seven school districts to take their first steps toward desegregation. Chief among them was the Central Alabama Citizens' Council, based in Montgomery and led by state senator Samuel Englehart, a wealthy planter from Macon County. An original board member of the Birmingham-based American States Rights Association, Englehart was named as secretary of the larger Association of Citizens' Councils created in February 1956, pledged to keep a respectable face on the battle for segregation.

Englehart's chief competitor was altogether different. Asa Earl Carter—"Ace" to his friends—was born on a small farm in Calhoun County, Alabama, on September 4, 1925. The eldest of four children, he was not orphaned in infancy as later claimed, but rather saw both parents survive well into his adulthood. Carter joined the U.S. Navy in World War II, was sent to learn radio broadcasting at the University of Colorado in Boulder, and returned in peacetime briefly to study journalism, leaving without a degree. After college, Carter served as an aide to Gerald L.K. Smith, then followed in Bull Connor's footsteps, working as a radio announcer in several states. By 1954, he was at Birmingham's station WILD, acting as spokesman for the American States Rights Association.

The ASRA and WILD severed that connection in February 1955, when he attacked the National Conference of Christians and Jews—founders of National Brotherhood Week—as part of an international communist conspiracy. Unfazed by that flub, Carter bounced back in October 1955 with the creation of his own North Alabama Citizen's Council.

If Sam Englehart represented upper-class racism, Carter's strident extremism set the North Alabama Council apart from its rivals. In the March 1956 issue of his newsletter, *The Southerner,* Carter himself described the kind of member he preferred:

> Through his veins flow the fire, the initiative, the stalwartness of the Anglo Saxon. Proof of his enviable reputation is the attack upon him. For such has been coined the words "red neck" and "wool hatter"..."cracker," and "hill billy." He has accepted the words rather than fought them...accepted them for what they are: For "red neck," takes mind of the toil beneath God's sun and with His good earth, of that he feels no shame; the "wool hat" has been his way, with little money, of wearing something "special" to God's house on Sunday morning; the "cracker" he adopts as his calling card of delicate cocksureness; and if "hilly billy" he be, then he exults in the high whine of the fiddle's bow that calls up the sound of the fierce Scot blood that sounded the bagpipe of battle and lamented in the ballads of yore.

Pledged to "keep the Council movement in the hands of the people" and "to prevent politicians and their front men from heading up our movement," Ace Carter blasted Englehart's CACC and the larger Alabama Association of Citizens' Councils for their "political chicanery" and "evasion," calling instead for dynamic opposition to "mongrelization, degradation, atheism, and communistic dictatorship." His councilors, Ace vowed, "are not playing for peace in our time....[W]e will fight it out for our children rather than pass the fight to them." Accused of anti-Semitism by Englehart's allies, Carter refuted the "utterly fantastic and hate hongering [*sic*] charge" as a fabrication by traitors who would "deny Jesus Christ in our movement."

Ace Carter harangues a gathering of his North Alabama Citizens' Council.
Credit: Library of Congress

One early recruit who answered Carter's call to arms was Robert Chambliss. On February 3, 1956, when black Birmingham co-ed Autherine Lucy won her three-year legal struggle to enroll at the state university in Tuscaloosa, Chambliss joined in a three-day series of campus riots, hurling rocks, eggs and firecrackers while chanting, "Keep 'Bama white!" and "Hey-hey, ho-ho, Autherine's got to go." University regents agreed on February 7, suspending Lucy indefinitely "for your safety and for the safety of students and faculty members."

Chambliss himself was one of four hooligans briefly jailed on charges of disorderly conduct during the campus riots, but no trial resulted. Instead, NAACP attorneys Arthur Shores and Thurgood Marshall accused Bob and his fellow jailbirds—Kenneth Thompson, Earl Watts, and brother Ed Watts—of conspiring and "acting in concert" with university administrators to obstruct court-ordered integration. Delighted by the free publicity, Chambliss and his cohorts fired back with a lawsuit against the NAACP, seeking four million dollars in damages. They saw no money for their efforts, but were satisfied when university regents expelled Lucy permanently for, as they claimed, making "outrageous, false and baseless accusations" of conspiracy. From the sidelines, ex-Klansman Hugh Locke described Thurgood Marshall as "a monkey trained to roller-skate."

Encouraged by that victory, Carter formally announced his council's separation from the AACC on March 5, then rallied 3,000 supporters on March 9 to demand Governor Folsom's impeachment "for failure to enforce segregation." March 30 brought a call from Carter's headquarters to ban rock-and-roll, which he deemed to be "sensuous Negro music" eroding the "entire moral structure of man, of Christianity, of spirituality in Holy marriage...of all the white man has built through his devotion to God." If anyone missed the point, Carter topped his latest broadside with the headline "Bebop Promotes Communism."

More specifically, Ace laid the blame for that musical assault on black singer and Montgomery, Alabama, native Nat "King" Cole. Carter branded Cole "a vicious agitator for integration," inflaming his councilors to the point that half a dozen of them leapt on stage to pummel Cole during a concert at Birmingham's Municipal Auditorium on April 10. Rather than disclaim the rowdy thugs, Carter blamed their victim and established a White People's Defense Fund to cover their legal expenses. The attackers were sentenced to six months in jail but apparently learned nothing. Ringleader Jesse Mabry would be back in headlines the following year, for an atrocity that sent him to state prison.

If some observers confused Carter's NACC with the Klan, it was no accident. A new Ku Klux faction was active in Birmingham, rallying 200 members in full regalia on August 25. *Jet* magazine subsequently described another meeting on November 15, where fifteen members took their oath before "a bonfire of human skulls," vowing to "fight the enemies of Jesus Christ to the bitter end and after." Interviewed by journalist John Barlow Martin, Ace Carter described the new Klan as an "important factor" in town. Pressed on the subject of personal membership, Carter smiled and replied, "I couldn't say if I was." Were any of his council members also Klansmen? "I haven't asked them," Carter said, "but I imagine quite a few are."

Rioters protest Autherine Lucy's admission to the University of Alabama.
Credit: Library of Congress

In fact, as circumstances soon made clear, Carter was the founding leader of the newly-formed Original Ku Klux Klan of the Confederacy, a rough-and-ready band that did not shy away from violence. As with the NACC previously, Robert Chambliss was among his first recruits. And already, Carter had his eye on battlefields beyond the city limits. He helped transient racist agitator Frederick John Kasper found the Virginia-based Seaboard White Citizens' Council and joined Kasper for a series of rallies that sparked rioting against school integration in Clinton, Tennessee, during September 1956. Some members of the AACC began describing Carter as a "Führer," proved at least partly correct when his troops replaced their robes with new brown-shirted uniforms.

If Carter hogged the local headlines during 1956 and '57, he was not alone by any means. The *Brown* decision had spawned at least five other Alabama Klans besides the OKKKC, with their number including:

The U.S. Klans, Knights of the Ku Klux Klan, Inc., founded in Georgia during May 1954 and chartered by the state in October 1955, led from Atlanta by Imperial Wizard Eldon Edwards, with klaverns in Alabama and seven other southern states.

The Gulf Coast Ku Klux Klan, composed of U.S. Klans defectors in Mobile and environs who left the parent group in autumn 1956. Its leader, gunsmith Elmo Barnard, was notorious for killing a black, fifteen-year-old burglar at his shop in September 1953. By January 1957, Mobile had witnessed twenty cross-burnings, three bombings, arson attacks on a black home and an elementary school, three black homes peppered by gunfire, and various rock-throwing incidents perpetrated by nightriders.

The Ku Klux Klan of the Confederacy, another U.S. Klans splinter group launched in 1956, unrelated to Ace Carter's group of similar name.

The Alabama Ku Klux Klan, Inc. and competing **Alabama Knights of the Ku Klux Klan**, both organized in 1957.

The Association of Alabama Knights of the Ku Klux Klan, also claiming scattered outposts in Mississippi.

The Dixie Ku Klux Klan, reported active in the 1950s by author Numan Bartley, though congressional investigators later pegged its start-up date as 1960.

Eldon Edwards, founder and "wizard" of the U.S. Klans.
Credit: Florida State Archives

Journalist Fletcher Knebel estimated total national Klan membership at 100,000 in April 1957, but accurate tallies were problematic, as usual. Aside from Ace Carter, Alabama's most visible Klansmen were Alvin Horn and a relative newcomer, Robert Marvin Shelton. An employee of the B.F. Goodrich tire plant in Tuscaloosa, born in 1929, Shelton joined the U.S. Klans under Horn, then replaced Horn as grand dragon after scandal engulfed the parson in June 1957. Specifically, the forty-five-year-old widower eloped with fifteen-year-old Barbara Richardson, described in press reports as "a pretty girl with peculiar eyes, one brown and the other blue." Richardson's parents filed for annulment of the marriage, then dropped their case when Barbara announced her pregnancy. Eldon Edwards, in Atlanta, hoped that Shelton would restore his Klan's good name and keep it on an even keel.

Montgomery and Mayhem

In December 1955, the focus of civil rights tension shifted to Alabama's capital, where African Americans led by Rev. Martin Luther King, Jr. had launched a boycott of segregated city buses. A Georgia native, six months older than his soon-to-be mortal enemy Robert Shelton, King soon became the focus of every Klansman's hatred, reviled in print and speeches as "Martin Lucifer Coon," branded a communist, and later tagged by aging FBI Director J. Edgar Hoover himself as "the most notorious liar in America."

Rev. Martin Luther King, Jr. removes a Klan cross from his yard in Montgomery, Alabama.
Credit: Library of Congress

The notion of a black boycott was shocking to white Alabamians in 1955 and '56. While police shadowed the boycott's leaders and Citizens' Council members published lists of participants' names, addresses, and phone numbers, encouraging harassment, members of the KKK took a more direct approach. From Birmingham, Ace Carter told reporters:

> If I were in Montgomery now, I'd be organizing an underground resistance.

Its purpose? "That," he smirked, "would be hard to say. I think somebody'd get killed." Alvin Horn agreed, declaring:

> The way I feel about Negroes who want to integrate is this: they don't want an education, they want a funeral.

Klansmen in the capital, it seemed, had similar ideas. A rash of bombings rocked the city, striking King's home and others, plus several black churches. Four Klansmen were belatedly charged with planting the bombs; white jurors acquitted two in May 1957, despite a signed confession, and the others were freed without trial in an amnesty also extended to boycott leaders—in short, the city's power structure equated peaceful black protest with white terrorism. And in the midst of all that mayhem, true to Ace Carter's prediction, someone was killed.

Rev. Ralph Abernathy (right) inspects bomb damage to his home in Montgomery, January 1957. *Credit: National Archives*

Inflamed by rumors that a black truck driver for the Winn-Dixie supermarket chain had "said something to offend a white woman," Montgomery Exalted Cyclops Walter Boyett ordered punitive action. On the night of January 23, 1957, four Klansmen kidnapped Winn-Dixie driver Willie Edwards, Jr. and, despite his tearful protestations of innocence, forced him at gunpoint to leap from a bridge spanning the Alabama River, where he drowned. A deathbed confession from Klansman Raymond Britt, Jr. prompted the 1976 arrest of three others—including notoriously violent Sonny Kyle Livingston, one of the acquitted 1957 bombers—but Judge Frank Embry dismissed the case on grounds that no cause of death was determined for Edwards.

Other acts of Ku Klux violence during 1957 included a home invasion at Maplesville, where six African American men were beaten with blackjacks; the whipping of four reputed NAACP members at Evergreen; the lashing of a black minister in Centreville; the flogging of a white man whom Klansmen accused of "associating too freely with Negroes"; and the beating of a press photographer at a Birmingham Klan rally. Ace Carter himself made headlines in January 1957, jailed on charges of shooting a fellow Klansman who objected to Carter's autocratic rule. Ace posted $20,000 bond pending trial, but his victim survived and the Klan leader never faced trial.

Aside from traditional nightriding, Birmingham Klansmen resumed their bombing campaign against blacks on December 25, 1956, blasting the parsonage of Bethel Baptist Church where activist Rev. Fred Lee Shuttlesworth served as a lightning rod for white hatred, on par with Dr. King in Montgomery. On New Year's Eve, a house newly purchased by blacks was demolished in Fountain Heights. Bob Chambliss set the charge, and was nearly abandoned when his nervous getaway driver fled prematurely, dragging Chambliss for a block before he managed to get in the car. On April 10, 1957, two days after black minister George Dickerson occupied his new Birmingham home, a dynamite blast wrecked the house. Eighteen days

Rev. Fred Shuttlesworth outside his parsonage, target of a Klan bombing in December 1956.
Credit: Library of Congress

later, another bomb rocked Bessemer's Allen Temple African Methodist Episcopal Church during an evening service, breaking windows and showering choir members with plaster. A second local bombing on the same day struck the home of a black labor leader. July saw another black-owned home dynamited in Birmingham.

Politics as Usual

Race was the main political issue in Alabama during 1956, and for many years thereafter. John Crommelin challenged incumbent Senator

Joseph Lister Hill in that year's Democratic primary, and while he failed to unseat Hill, the openly-racist ex-admiral received thirty-two percent of the popular vote—115,440 ballots to Hill's winning 247,519.

Bull Connor, sidelined since 1953, still had another year to wait before he sought office again. In the run-up to 1957's municipal elections, Commissioner of Public Safety Robert Lindbergh faced competition from ex-commissioner Wade Bradley, union official Joe Captain, and lately-arrested Klan chieftain Ace Carter. The *Birmingham News* endorsed Lindbergh, but Connor appealed to hard-line segregationists with a promise that he would not allow "professional agitators and radicals to come into Birmingham and stir up racial strife. I'll enforce the law twenty-four hours a day throughout my term."

Which law that might be remained open to question. Lindbergh, without mentioning Connor by name, told voters:

> My first official act as the elected head of the Police Department was to remove the press gat [*sic*] that had heretofore clothed the activities of this department in a veil of secrecy, through which the truth was shining only dimly and sometimes not at all.

On primary day, Lindbergh polled 14,238 votes to Connor's 11,938, but his failure to win a majority forced a runoff vote. Perhaps with Montgomery's troubles in mind, voters turned out in large numbers, and Connor squeaked to victory over Lindbergh by a margin of 103 ballots. When no Republican contender surfaced for the general election in November, Bull was victorious.

And none too soon, in the minds of local Klansmen. Congress had passed a new Civil Rights Act on September 9, 1957, and President Dwight Eisenhower had sent troops to integrate Central High School in Little Rock, Arkansas, two weeks later. Appalled at that move, Connor told reporters:

> It is clear to me that he [Eisenhower] is wrong, and I am one of those who believe that right will triumph. Since we are right—both morally and legally—in this matter, let's be stout-hearted and firm in the defense of the laws of Alabama and the ordinances of the City of Birmingham.

One obstacle to that end, as Bull saw it, was Police Chief Jamie Moore, a twenty-one-year veteran of the department appointed as chief on May 6, 1956. During the recent primary election, Moore had spoken disdainfully of Connor, telling associates, "We don't want that loudmouth talking up and down the halls." Soon after his inauguration, Connor told Moore, "You don't fit into the picture as my chief of police," adding, "I hear you have not been enforcing the law." Strapped for specifics, Bull sought to oust Moore on charges of "political activity and waste of city property," but the city personnel board exonerated Moore in January 1958. After several months of petty harassment, Connor finally made peace with Moore and the chief kept his job, though Bull would still run things himself where race and Klan collaboration were concerned.

Judge Aaron

Ace Carter's Klansmen made their last and most atrocious foray on September 2, 1957, when six members kidnapped black handyman Edward "Judge" Aaron from suburban Zion City, driving him back to their klavern in East Lake. There, they beat, kicked, pistol-whipped, and grilled Aaron about his nonexistent civil rights activities before Exalted Cyclops Joe Pritchett told him:

> I want you to carry a message to Shuttlesworth. We're gonna take your life or your nuts. You got your choice. Which will it be?

When Aaron could not choose between death and castration, Prichett made the choice for him. The Klansmen pinned their victim to the dirt floor of the klavern meeting house, stripped off his pants, and Pritchett handed a razor blade to prospective Klan officer Bart Floyd with the command: "Do your duty." Floyd severed Aaron's scrotum, then doused the wound with turpentine to elicit more screams. Prichett passed around the "evidence" of Floyd's achievement in a paper cup, receiving a unanimous vote for Floyd's installment as captain (a rank unknown to most Klans).

Next, the Klansmen dragged Aaron back to their car, drove him some eight miles from the crime scene, and dumped him beside the highway. In the process, they forgot their cup of "evidence," sitting on the shoulder of the road, and came back to retrieve it. Aaron, fearing that they had returned to kill him, crawled and staggered to concealment in a nearby creek bed, then made his way back to the road when the Klansmen departed for good. Police later received a passing motorist's report of a "bloody Negro" lurching along the highway and patrolmen responded, transporting Aaron to Birmingham's Veterans Administration Medical Center, where surgeons saved his life. Meanwhile, nightriders burned ten crosses the same night, at public schools in Bessemer and western Jefferson County.

Although inured to racial violence, most white Birminghamians were outraged by Aaron's ordeal. State police, led by investigator Ben Allen, soon found the klavern, its floor stained with blood and turpentine. Allen interrogated klavern members until two of the kidnappers—John Griffin and William Miller—confessed and named the rest: Pritchett and Floyd, Grover McCullough, and Jesse Mabry, one of Nat "King" Cole's 1956 assailants. Ben Allen, himself a strict segregationist who drew a line between "good niggers" and agitators, faced the Klansmen in his office and warned them, as he later said, that if "they didn't have just cause, they'd better find 'em a damn rock to git under, because I was gonna git 'em."

Allen's investigation of Edward Aaron soon revealed that no "just cause" existed. Aaron was neither a civil rights worker nor rapist; in fact, every Caucasian who knew him described him to Allen as an amiable "white folks' nigger." Allen charged the six Klansmen with mayhem—defined by Alabama law as the unlawful, malicious and intentional disabling or severance of any victim's body parts, with penalties ranging from two to twenty years in prison. He warned the six defendants to expect the maximum.

Frightened, Griffin and Miller struck a deal with prosecutor Walter Perry. Both turned state's evidence against their fellow Klansmen, trading testimony for five-year prison terms, suspended in exchange for probation based on their cooperation with police. At trial before Judge Alta King in November 1957, Mabry and McCullough insisted that they thought Pritchett and Floyd only meant to "scare the nigger" without harming him. Jurors convicted all four, and Judge King imposed the maximum twenty-year sentence on each, declaring for the record that "[t]here has never been a case in all my years of law practice and ten years on the bench that has shocked me as this one has."

Appeals stalled execution of the sentences for two more years, some Klansmen still convinced that the guilty defendants would never serve time, but all were imprisoned by late 1959. In 1960, the state's parole board ruled that all four should serve at least one-third of the twenty years imposed before they were considered for release. In theory, none should have been freed before the summer of 1966—but once again, as we shall see, racism would contrive to bend the rules.

If nothing else, the Aaron case *did* spell the end for Ace Carter's Original KKK of the Confederacy. By early 1958, his faction had dissolved, its diehard members scattered into other Klans, while some departed from the fold for good. Embarrassed by publicity surrounding Aaron's mutilation and his own arrest for shooting fellow Klansmen, Carter faded from the public eye, but he was not defeated yet. Given some time and distance from the battleground of Birmingham, he would resurface four years later at the elbow of the state's most famous and most controversial governor.

Ace Carter (left) scuffles with detectives seeking to arrest him for shooting two Klansmen.
Credit: National Archives

Chapter 4
The Sting

Despite the bombing of his home and the Ku Klux "message" sent to him via Edward Aaron's castration, Rev. Fred Shuttlesworth refused to step back from the front lines of civil rights work. Born in Montgomery County, Alabama, on March 18, 1922, Shuttlesworth had been raised in rural Oxmoor, close to Birmingham. He drove a truck at Mobile's Brookley Army Air Field—now Mobile Downtown Airport—during World War II, then felt a "calling" to the ministry and enrolled at nearby Cedar Grove Bible College. Further study at Selma University (another Baptist school) and all-black Alabama State College led Shuttlesworth to serve as pastor at Selma's First Baptist Church in 1952, but his style unnerved conservative deacons. The following year, Shuttlesworth found his niche at Bethel Baptist Church in north Birmingham.

Unwilling to stand idly by while segregation oppressed his people, the new pastor quickly joined in NAACP campaigns to register black voters, and in Civic League drives to clean up local bars. In June 1956, after racist Alabama legislators banned the NAACP from operating inside the state, Shuttlesworth founded an Alabama Christian Movement for Human Rights (ACMHR) to take up the slack. His tireless advocacy for racial equality prompted Klansmen to bomb his parsonage on Christmas 1956. Ten weeks later, on March 5, 1957, a white man assaulted Shuttlesworth and his wife, Ruby, after they entered the "white" waiting room of Birmingham's railroad depot.

"We're Making Progress"

Four days after the attack on Edward Aaron, and before his mutilators were arrested, Jefferson County's board of education considered Shuttleworth's petition to integrate all-white Phillips High School, but refused to make a decision. "It would be foolish," the superintendent declared, "to decide before an investigation is completed." Shuttlesworth saw the run-around for what it was and issued a televised statement revealing his plan to enroll black students at Phillips High on September 9—the same day President Eisenhower was scheduled to sign the new Civil Rights Act.

That Tuesday morning, Rev. J.S. Phifer—vice president of the ACMHR and another target of Ku Klux harassment—drove Shuttlesworth and his wife to the high school, accompanied by their two daughters and two other black students, Nathaniel Lee and Walter Wilson. Forewarned by the minister's press conference, an estimated twenty Klansmen waited at the school, armed with chains, brass knuckles, and clubs. Klan wives formed a cheering section on the sidelines. Nearby, assembled journalists noted a frowning observer "who looked like Ace Carter."

As Shuttlesworth stepped from the car, the Klansmen rushed forward, pulled the minister's jacket over his head, and began to beat him. One shouted, "We've got the son of a bitch now! Let's kill him!" The Klan wives concurred, one calling out, "Kill the motherfucker now and it will all be over!" Other thugs smashed the car's windows, and one opened the driver's door, flailing at J.S. Phifer with a chain, whereupon Phifer struck back with what he later called "a nonviolent right hook." Ruby Shuttlesworth moved to help her husband and received a stab wound to her hip.

Several minutes into the attack, police belatedly arrived. News cameras rolled as "half a dozen motor scouts and four patrol cars moved [in] as if by prearrangement." The tardy officers arrested three Klansmen—J.E. Breckenridge, W.J. "Jack" Cash, and Ivey Ford Gauldin—while the others fled. Fred Shuttlesworth, barely conscious, lurched back to the car and Phifer sped away toward University Hospital. There, as reported in the *Birmingham News*, police dispersed "curious groups" of a hundred or more whites while Shuttlesworth entered the hospital on a stretcher. Physicians found that he had suffered minor kidney damage, a sprained arm, plus various cuts and bruises.

"You must have a hard skull," one examiner remarked.

"Doctor," Shuttlesworth replied, "the Lord knew I was in a hard town, so He gave me a hard head."

Before departing from the hospital, police searched Rev. Phifer and discovered a .25-caliber pistol. Phifer explained his fear of Klan assaults, but all in vain. On September 21, he was charged with carrying a concealed firearm and assorted traffic violations. At the same time, officers explained their late arrival at Phillips High: a "prank" call timed to coincide with the attack on Shuttlesworth, reporting a stolen car, had delayed them. The vehicle in question was registered to Bull Connor.

Fred Shuttlesworth, meanwhile, left University Hospital the same afternoon he was beaten, brushing off one physician's concern with the remark, "Doc, we're making progress." Outside, he told reporters:

> I believe I have been sent to lead God's army in our fight for freedom, as today is the second time within a year that a miracle has spared my life.

Appearing before a grand jury on September 19, Klansmen Cash, Gaudin, and Breckenridge denied assaulting Shuttlesworth or anyone else at Phillips High School. Arresting officers declined to identify them, and the panel ignored news photographs of the attack. On October 5, the grand jury issued a no-bill in Shuttlesworth's case. Eighteen days later, nightriding Klansmen burned five crosses in the black district of Prattville, sixty-seven miles south of Birmingham.

Defiance and Dynamite

Fred Shuttlesworth's ACMHR was not the only group of "agitators" active in Birmingham. The Alabama Council for Human Relations (ACHR), a local chapter of the older Georgia-based Southern Regional Council, also worked tirelessly under Dr. Robert Hughes toward racial parity. Relocated from Gadsden to Birmingham in 1956, after white landlords drove Dr. Hughes from his medical office, the ACHR had suffered little opposition from police under Commissioner Robert Lindbergh, but that was about to change.

Bull Connor, happily reunited with his "stolen" car, had yet to resume his commission seat when police moved against the ACHR in October 1957, invading one of its meetings with backup from burly white civilians whom Dr. Hughes assumed to be Klansmen. Within days, the employers and neighbors of ACHR members received anonymous letters branding the group's adherents as communists. One of the fifty-odd who tendered resignations from the group to Dr. Hughes thereafter was William Miller, recent ex-Klansman and one of Edward Aaron's repentant abductors.

November 1957 found Bull Connor back in office, launching his abortive campaign to oust Police Chief Jamie Moore. Robert Chambliss dusted off his police radio, racing to the scene of calls from Birmingham's black neighborhoods, sometimes arriving first and pistol-whipping black "suspects" before patrolmen arrived. The officers seemed to appreciate his efforts, perhaps—as former acting chief Jack Warren acknowledged, thirty years later—because "one or two" policemen were dues-paying Klansman, while "the majority" of Connor's force sympathized with Klan tactics and goals.

Despite those outings, Chambliss still had time for more bombings. In the predawn hours of December 7, 1957, two blasts wrecked a home newly purchased by blacks in Fountain Heights. Fire Marshal Aaron Rosenfeld called the bombing Birmingham's worst yet, explaining that it had been staged "more skillfully than previous explosions." Various reports called it the district's fourth blast, or Birmingham's seventh, within a year. An article published in the journal *New South*, six years later, cited *five* local bombings in December 1957 alone, but offered no substantiating details.

Whatever the tally, Bull Connor branded the latest attack "a terrible thing," vowing that his detectives would "do all we can to find the person or persons who did this and send them to the penitentiary." The thrust of his supposed investigation was revealed on December 8, when Connor placed the blame on real estate agents who sold homes to blacks. "They know when they sell these houses that it is liable to cause trouble," he said, "and the Negroes themselves should know not to buy those homes." As a deterrent, he proposed that Birmingham's Real Estate Board revoke the licenses of any agents who encouraged residential integration "before somebody gets killed." Bull further ordered the shattered home's owners to repair their dwelling within thirty days, or see it condemned and bulldozed. While that sideshow went on, an FBI informant advised bureau headquarters that "Connor did not intend to solve this bombing."

Having scored their most destructive bombing thus far in December, Birmingham Klansmen fumbled in their next two attempts. On February 20, 1958, a bomb left at a local black church failed to explode and was found by parishioners, delivered to apathetic police. Two months later, on April 28, rain doused the fuse attached to fifty-four sticks of dynamite planted on Birmingham's south side, at the Temple Beth-El synagogue. Bull Connor called upon the FBI to take that case and run with it, a bid that bureau memos branded an attempt "to unload his investigative responsibilities, in connection with the bombings."

"All Integration Must Stop"

The day before Birmingham's latest dud was discovered, two bombs exploded in Jacksonville, Florida, damaging a black school and an all-white synagogue. Rabbi Sanders Tofield received a phone call from an individual who introduced himself as "General Ponce de Leon," commander of "The Confederate Underground." The caller warned Tofield that all Jews must evacuate the state of Florida, except Miami Beach, or face extinction. A second call to Jacksonville authorities advised:

> We have just blown up a Jewish center of integration. Every segregationist in the South must go free. All integration must stop.

Neither the "general" nor any of his followers would ever be identified, but one Floridian who sympathized felt free to speak in public. Klan leader Bill Hendrix advised his knights:

> Now, I don't want you good people to go around blowin' up buildings or temples, but the next time somebody does blow up a temple, I sure hope it is filled with Jews.

April's bombings capped an epidemic of explosions in Dixie. One account, published on December 31, 1954, claimed l95 racist bombings and arson attacks in the eight months following the *Brown* decision. A more modest accounting, by author Barbara Patterson in *New South*, listed 143 bombings across the South—with one fatality, in Georgia— since January 1956. Whatever the accurate tally, certain southern law enforcement officers now felt compelled to do what J. Edgar Hoover's "G-men" refused to attempt.

On May 3, 1958, officials from twenty-eight southern cities gathered in Jacksonville to create the Southern Conference on Bombing, a "clearing house" for information leading to arrest and prosecution of Dixie's hyperactive terrorists. Bull Connor attended the meeting, where ex-FBI agent Milton Ellerin, lately employed by the Anti-Defamation League of B'nai B'rith, distributed a list of notorious anti-Semites likely to participate in synagogue bombings. That list named Robert Chambliss, castrator Bart Floyd, recently-deposed Birmingham Exalted Cyclops Troy Ingram—and "Connor, Eugene (Bull)." While other lawmen tried to hide their mocking grins, Ellerin apologized for the "clerical error." Red-faced Bull voted with the other delegates to authorize rewards totaling $55,700 for information breaking any of Dixie's recent headline-grabbing blasts. Tips were received, but none panned out. The cash was safe. No bombers were arrested.

But in Bull's case, for the first time ever, it was not for lack of trying.

Stinging Stoner

Three days after the Jacksonville conference, having missed its point entirely, the *Birmingham News* ran a headline asking: "Are Reds Behind Bombings?" The subhead reported that "J. Edgar Hoover Says Communists Are Exploiting Race Issues on a National Scale." And while Hoover had been peddling that line since 1917, Bull Connor understood that he needed a more realistic scapegoat.

Potential salvation arrived in Bull's office on May 8, in the person of retired Klan leader William Morris. According to Connor, in a statement recorded two months later, Morris said:

> Mr. Connor, I believe I can tell you who put that dynamite at the Temple Beth-El and at the Jewish synagogue in Jacksonville. If he didn't do it, he is the kingpin who had it done....I want to get a promise out of you on the square that you will never mention my name to anyone because this is the most dangerous man that I have ever known....This man will do anything against the Jews and the Negroes, and especially against the Jews. He hates the Jews.

As Connor told the tale, Morris:

> ...went along in his conversation explaining to me on the numerous occasions when he had met him and how wild he was. Sometimes he would get so excited talking to him about the Jews that he would have to quiet him down so that the people across the street from his house could not hear him. He also told me the name of the organization that he thought he headed up, of which there were not over six or eight members....He said that this man has an alibi for every bombing that he has ever had anything to do with....He told me this fellow's name was J.B. Stoner.

Jesse Stoner at National States Rights Party headquarters.
Credit: National Archives

The group in question was a fledgling neo-Nazi clique, the National States Rights Party (NSRP), whose founders included John Crommelin, Frederick John Kasper, future American Nazi Party leader George Lincoln Rockwell, and various Klan leaders. The upshot of Connor's meeting with Morris: a plot to entrap, arrest, and prosecute Stoner as Birmingham's lone bomber, thus clearing local Klansmen.

While that plot was brewing, on June 3, Fred Shuttlesworth confronted the city commission with another petition for school integration. Connor accused the minister of doing "more to set your people back than any man in the history of this city," adding, "I wouldn't vote for nothing for you." After the meeting, Connor told reporters that his detectives suspected Shuttlesworth of bombing his own church in 1956. With that in mind, Bull suggested that police give Shuttlesworth a polygraph test "to clear up some of the rumors that have been circulating." Shuttlesworth replied that he would gladly take the test if Connor did likewise, with questions addressing Klan membership, Bull's hatred of blacks, and rampant police corruption. Connor predictably refused, but told the media, "I am not and never have been" a Klansman.

On June 14, 1958, Jesse Stoner visited Birmingham, touring the city in a car borrowed from William Morris. He stopped at Bethel Baptist Church and asked to speak with Shuttlesworth, who was not in. When asked his business with the pastor, Stoner said, "I want him to pray for me. I'm in trouble." After surveying the church, Stoner offered to bomb it for $2,000. He also suggested a discount rate of $1,000 per bomb, if Morris picked two more targets.

Morris passed the message to police, who signaled their agreement to proceed. On June 21, again driving Morris's car, Stoner met two supposed local steelworkers—in fact, police Captain G.L. Pattie and Sergeant Tom Cook. The officers were wired for sound, with another detective and a sound technician recording every word from a nearby pickup truck. Other observers of the meeting, parked within sight of the motel, included Bull Connor, local FBI Special Agent in Charge (and future bureau director) Clarence Kelley, and two of Kelley's agents.

Captain Pattie described the substance of his conversation with Stoner in an official report that read:

> I opened the conversation with the remark that I had lately come into this local activity, that I had been opposed for many years to any violence, but for the past three years local conditions continued to be so bad among the negroes; that Rev. Shuttlesworth and Lamar Weaver had gone to the Terminal Station and sat in the White Waiting Room and were protected by the police....I stated that we had elected Commissioner Connor hoping that he would do something about the negro situation and that we were a little disappointed in him....Mr. "S" commented that all the politicians were influenced by the growing negro vote. Sergeant Cook and I told Mr. "S" that all the people here had left it up to us to decide in selecting a responsible person who would arrange for Rev. Shuttlesworth's church to be blown completely off the map and not leave a brick standing. We also told Mr. "S" that we didn't have quite enough money at this time, but that there were some big business people that had promised to come through with some substantial donations to the cause, but that they must be satisfied that it would be a thorough and complete job and not a dud, such as was set off at the Bethel Jewish Church....Mr. "S"'s reply was that 54 sticks of dynamite would certainly have destroyed the building, but that perhaps (and he smiled when he said this) "the Jews were attempting to raise money."
>
> ...I stated to him that I did not want to know who would set the bomb, that I had been told by the informer [Morris] that he, Mr. "S" could have it arranged for $2,000. Mr. "S" agreed that he could have the church completely destroyed for $2,000....I told Mr. "S" that we hoped the

total destruction of the church would persuade Shuttlesworth to leave Birmingham and go up North where he belonged, but if that did not work our group would be willing to go further with another job that would eliminate Rev. Shuttlesworth completely. Mr. "S"'s reply was that some people would set out bombs and some would do the other type of work, but he could arrange either or both type jobs. Sergeant Cook then explained again that we did not have the $2,000 but we had a few hundred....We promised to let Mr. "S" know, by contacting the informer, when we would have the $2,000 needed and told him we were sure we would have the money within the next ten days or two weeks....

Through the whole interview with Mr. "S" he was careful to avoid any incriminating admission about any past acts. We mentioned that the damage to the Jewish church in Jacksonville was very slight and we wanted a complete job. He only smiled as he did in discussing the failure of the bomb to go off at Bethel in Birmingham.

When discussing the possibility of Shuttlesworth not leaving Birmingham after his church was destroyed, Mr. "S" reminded [us] that several years ago two negro NAACP leaders in Florida were blown up and eliminated, and he smiled when he mentioned this....

Mr. "S" stated that he had seen the bomb and it was made up and could be brought to Birmingham on short notice....He also said that any bomb that was put down and did not explode that we would not be charged for it, but another would be set off.

Captain Pattie's written statement is the only surviving record of his conversation with Stoner on June 21. Connor later claimed that the tape-recorder malfunctioned, though author Diane McWhorter suggests the recording was destroyed deliberately. A possible reason: twenty years later, Stoner told the House Select Committee on Assassinations that Morris had offered him $25,000 to kill Rev. Martin Luther King Jr. in Montgomery. The same offer, he said, was made to Ace Carter, described in the committee's final report as "a Stoner associate." Morris "vehemently denied" the accusation, although FBI reports cited his call for King's assassination at a 1961 Klan meeting.

[Dr. King was later assassinated, in April 1968. The FBI's investigation of that murder—and a subsequent review by the U.S. House Select Committee on Assassinations ten years later—found no links between the Klan and King's slaying. Nonetheless, two attorneys retained by King's alleged assassin, James Earl Ray, were Arthur Hanes, Sr. and Jesse

Stoner, both longtime defenders of indicted Klansmen, both identified in various reports (though unconfirmed, in Hanes's case) as members of the KKK. A Klansman called before the House Committee also testified that Robert Shelton's UKA hired Hanes to represent Ray in court. Hanes denied it, saying the UKA retainer was paid for his defense of several North Carolina Klansmen charged with murder in an unrelated case.]

Well aware of the Klan's unhealthy interest in their church, armed Bethel Baptist parishioners stood watch around the clock. On Sunday, June 29, police surprised the guards and confiscated four of their guns. Around the same time, a detective on duty at Birmingham's Greyhound bus depot saw Stoner arrive with fellow NSRP member Robert Bowling, from Atlanta. Late that night, church deacon and lookout Will Hall found a five-gallon paint can hissing and smoking against Bethel Baptist's east wall. He carried it to a roadside ditch, then ran for his life as the bomb exploded, shattering windows of the church and nearby homes. Coincidentally or otherwise, the first two officers to reach the site were Stoner's contacts, Sergeant Cook and Captain Pattie.

Allegedly shocked by the blast, Connor claimed that one of his officers:

> ...called our informer long distance...and told him of the bombing and asked him if he thought Stoner had had anything to do with it, and he said no he didn't believe so. About twenty minutes later, our informer called back and said Stoner had just called long distance and told him that they had bombed this church and he wanted him to get some money out of us for the job. Our man told our informer that we had never told him that we *would* give him money to bomb any place or church. We said we *might* could get some people to give us some money. He said he told Stoner that those people had not told him that we would give him any money to bomb this church.

Clearly, Connor's latest statement—contradicting Captain Pattie's—was a bid to protect himself and his department. In addition to Pattie's affidavit, Diane McWhorter writes that the officers *had* given Stoner $100 on June 21, "to cover his expenses so far." In any case, all sides agree that he received no further payment for the bombing. Neither was he prosecuted, since Birmingham's district attorney feared allegations of entrapment. Police returned the confiscated guns to Bethel Baptist members on June 30, while Will Hall and five other guards took polygraph tests to prove that they were "victims only—not plotters or conspirators."

Bethel Baptist Church, target of a police-orchestrated bombing in June 1958.
Credit: Library of Congress

Still fearing implication in the bombing, Connor turned to the feds. As he described the situation in his statement of July 16:

> There is no question in my mind after reading [Cook's and Pattie's] statements and talking with my informer for eight hours Sunday that we have just about come to the end and we have got to have help from the FBI to catch [Stoner] because he or his crowd do not live in the state of Alabama and we do not have men that we can put on to tail him 24 hours a day. I think this is one man who must be tailed every hour until he is caught or he and his crowd are going to do a lot of damage in the Southeast.

Fred Shuttlesworth was also writing to the FBI, urging its agents to "at least look into this problem of improper protection and other problems mentioned in this letter." Privately, he told colleagues, "Bull Connor finally made the mistake we have been waiting for. We've got him where we want him now." That hope was premature, but FBI headquarters got the message. A memo from Washington, dated July 24, ordered SAC Clarence Kelley "to hold contacts with Connor to a minimum because of his unsavory background."

"Harmless Explosions"

One day after Connor dictated his statement and called for federal assistance, terrorists struck again on Dynamite Hill. That night, July 17, Ernest Coppins saw four white men crouched in the dark outside his house, striking matches to light a bomb's fuse, and called out for help from his neighbors. The bomb exploded, causing no damage except to the Klansmen, whose getaway driver fled and left them stranded. Black residents surrounded Ellis Lee and Cranford Neal, pummeling both, stabbing Lee in one leg and slashing Neal's back before police arrived to rescue the Klansmen.

While the brawl was going on, a second bomb shattered the porch and front wall of William Blackwell's home nearby, debris gashing the neck of a child sleeping inside. The blast also damaged a white neighbor's home. Patrolmen cruising past that scene found a third suspect, Herbert Eugene Wilcutt, wandering about as if lost in the dark.

In custody, the trio admitted planning to bomb four or five houses after a KKK meeting where liquor flowed freely, but their plot was scotched by Ernest Coppins and the premature explosion of their first charge. Meanwhile, still at large in Birmingham, their getaway driver—Robert Chambliss—was boasting to friends that the bomb he had thrown "wasn't a dud." Detectives hauled him in for questioning, and while he still had wits enough to lie about the bombing, Chambliss later complained that he was treated "worse than a goddamn nigger" in jail.

The *Birmingham News* made light of the latest bombings, passing them off as "harmless explosions" that were "probably" set off by blacks, reserving editorial concern for the fact that Negroes had "ganged up" on whites. That argument collapsed on August 1, when Detective T.E. Lindsey recited confessions from Lee, Neal, and Wilcutt in a Jefferson County courtroom, prompting the judge to order all three held without bond pending trial. It seemed to be a dark day for the Klan, but this was still Birmingham.

Herbert Wilcutt was the first of the three to face trial, and the first local Klansmen ever indicted on bombing charges. Jurors convicted him on December 9, 1958, and fixed his sentence at ten years in prison— then recommended probation, instead. Wilcutt's judge was happy to oblige. Prosecutors then dismissed all charges against Lee and Neal. Bob Chambliss, although fuming at his treatment in the lockup, faced no charges and was free to bomb another day.

Even when Klansmen were arrested in commission of a crime and signed confessions, they appeared to be untouchable.

Chapter 5
Invisible Empires

While Bull Connor baited his trap for Jesse Stoner and drunken Klansmen raided Dynamite Hill, Alabama prepared to elect its next governor. The clear favorite in a field of fourteen Democratic contenders was John Malcolm Patterson, the state's attorney general. His closest competition, George Corley Wallace, Jr., was a protégé of Big Jim Folsom and circuit judge in Barbour County, where he set conflicting precedents by calling black witnesses "Mister" and issuing Dixie's first injunction against removal of segregation signs in railroad terminals. Other contenders included John Crommelin, lately a founder of the neo-Nazi National States Rights Party, and lawyer Ralph "Shorty" Price (best known for multiple arrests over his antics at Crimson Tide football games), a former college roommate of George Wallace.

Born in 1921, a second-generation attorney, John Patterson showed no interest in politics until June 18, 1954, when Phenix City gangsters murdered his father. On the day he died, Albert Patterson had won the Democratic primary race for attorney general, vowing to clean out the Mob. Sentimental voters elected son John in his place, and Patterson fielded National Guard troops to clean out Phenix City's vice dens.

John Patterson enlisted Klan help to win Alabama's 1958 gubernatorial election.
Credit: Library of Congress

In May 1956, he won the hearts of segregationists by filing an injunction that barred the NAACP—"a foreign corporation" that had failed to register with the secretary of state—from operating inside Alabama's borders. In 1958, he merged his best-known victories, claiming that "outside agitators" from the underworld and the NAACP had joined forces to defeat him.

But Patterson still needed help from the Klan. On March 19, 1958, he mailed scores of letters typed on his official stationery and addressed to Klansmen statewide. The message read:

Dear Mr. *****

A mutual friend, Mr. R.M. (Bob) Shelton, of ours in Tuscaloosa has suggested that I write to you and ask for your support in the coming Governor's race.

I hope you will see fit to support my candidacy and I would like to meet you when I am next in *****.

With warm personal regards, I am

Sincerely your friend,

/s/John Patteron
JOHN PATTERSON
Attorney General

The *Montgomery Advertiser* obtained one of Patterson's letters and gave it a front-page airing on May 15, whereupon Patterson loudly denied any ties to the Klan. "This is amazing," he proclaimed. "I am not a member of the Ku Klux Klan. I have never been a member. I don't know anyone named Shelton." Privately, however, Patterson told friends that Klansmen would "work all night nailing up signs, putting out literature." As for rival campaign signs, "They can also tear 'em down in one night. I wasn't about to run 'em off." Rumors persisted that the attorney general held regular meetings with KKK leaders.

Klansmen got the message and rallied for Patterson on June 3, the same day Bull Connor and Fred Shuttlesworth traded challenges for a polygraph test. Patterson won 196,859 votes to Wallace's 162,435, while the rest of the field divided the remaining 259,388. John Crommelin limped across the finish line with 2,245 votes, and Shorty Price trailed the pack with 655. (In a sideshow to the main event, Ace Carter joined the primary race for lieutenant governor, finishing last in a field of five hopefuls.)

Robert Shelton, ally and confidante of Alabama governors. *Credit: Library of Congress*

Since no candidate had scored a clear majority, state law required a run-off between Patterson and Wallace, scheduled for June 24. With Klansmen openly endorsing Patterson, George Wallace made a bid for Alabama's 75,000 black votes. He offered no relief from segregation, but observed that "Patterson chatters about the gangster ghosts of Phenix City while he himself is rolling with the new wave of the Klan and its terrible tradition of lawlessness." There were, Wallace noted, "a lot of pistol-toters and toughs among Klansmen." Leavening his message with humor, Wallace toured the state in a pickup truck, hauling a bed. In each village, he lifted the blankets while calling out, "Where is John Patterson? Who's down there between the sheets with you, John?"

All in vain. On June 24, Patterson polled 315,353 votes to Wallace's 250,451. Curiously, Patterson's tally in the November 3 general election was smaller, only 234,583 votes, but he still crushed Republican contender William Longshore (with 30,415) and independent rival William Jackson (with 903). George Wallace got the message, telling friends:

John Patterson out-niggered me. And boys, I won't be out-niggered again.

George Wallace criticized the Klan in 1958, later making it his ally.
Credit: Florida State Archives

Any doubts concerning Patterson's alliance with the KKK were soon erased. Following his January 1959 inauguration, Robert Shelton was promoted from the B.F. Goodrich assembly line to serve as the company's state sales agent, landing a $1.6 million contract to furnish tires for state vehicles. Around the same time, Patterson appointed Klansman Walter Brower as chairman of Jefferson County's Board of Registrars, a post that Brower used to purge black voters from the county rolls.

A Khaos of Klans

While Robert Shelton's ties to the governor's mansion boosted his status in Cotton State Klandom, his realm of the U.S. Klans faced competition from rivals and suffered dissent from within. On September 27, 1958, Mobile County Sheriff Ray Bridges announced the arrest of seven Klansmen—including Saraland Chief of Police N.W. "Pat" Patrick—in connection with a spate of local cross-burnings.

Seven months later, Klansmen armed with rifles waylaid three black employees of Birmingham's Hayes Aircraft Corporation (now Pemco Aeroplex Inc.) as they left work at 1 a.m. on April 10, 1959. Two of the captives were quickly released, while the kidnappers singled out Rev. Charles Billups, an A.M.E. pastor, winner of a Congressional Medal of Honor in the Korean War, and a member of Fred Shuttlesworth's Alabama Christian Movement for Human Rights. Driving Billups into the woods, they grilled him about the ACMHR's future plans, beat him with chains, then tied him to a tree and branded his stomach with the letters "KKK." Surviving that ordeal, Billups later told Shuttlesworth, "I felt sorry for them." So, apparently, did one of his attackers. When the repentant Klansmen visited Billups at home, announcing his plans to contact police and confess, Billups suggested that they pray together, instead.

In September 1959 the *New York Times* took notice of growing Klan strength in Alabama. Three months later, officials in Monroeville canceled the town's Christmas parade after Klansmen threatened violence over the inclusion of a black high school's marching band. In March 1960, police in Anniston detained a dozen Klansmen for questioning related to cross-burnings and a dynamite explosion in a black family's yard.

Robert Shelton enjoyed the publicity, but some of his own knights concerned him. Birmingham's largest klavern—formerly named for Robert E. Lee, now known as Eastview No. 13—included bombers Robert Chambliss, Thomas Blanton, Jr., and Bobby Frank Cherry—a proud participant in the September 1957 beating of Fred Shuttlesworth at Phillips High School. Shelton did not oppose such acts in principle; rather, his chief complaint was fraternization between Eastview Klansmen and the brown-shirted National States Rights Party.

Granted, Shelton was an anti-Semite in his own right, pleased to tell one interviewer that "I don't hate niggers, but I hate the Jews. The nigger's a child, but the Jews are dangerous people." That said, he drew the line at joining forces with overt fascists, such as the NSRP or George Lincoln Rockwell's new American Nazi Party. A descendant of Klansmen, Shelton was old enough to remember the embarrassment suffered from joint rallies held with the German-American Bund. A further indication of the danger inherent in flirting with Nazis came on October 12, 1958, when bombers struck a synagogue in Atlanta, Georgia.

"We Have Just Blown Up the Temple"

At 3:30 a.m. that day, a blast described as "expert" by police, ripped an eighteen-square-foot hole in one wall of Atlanta's oldest and wealthiest synagogue, commonly known as The Temple. Fifteen minutes later, United Press International received a phone call from "General Gordon of the Confederate Underground," stating:

> We bombed a temple in Atlanta. This is the last empty building in Atlanta that we will bomb. All nightclubs refusing to fire their Negro employees will also be blown up. We are going to blow up all communist organizations. Negroes and Jews are hereby declared aliens.

Police inspect bomb damage at an Atlanta synagogue, October 1958.
Credit: Library of Congress

Authorities never identified "General Gordon"—presumably a reference to Confederate Major General John Brown Gordon, Georgia's first grand dragon of the Reconstruction-era Klan, later governor of Georgia and a member of the U.S. Senate—but police knew where to look for local Jew-haters. Attorney Jesse Stoner lived nearby, sharing an office with James Venable, "imperial klonsel" (counsel) for the U.S. Klans. Stoner's latest brainchild, the NSRP, sang the same tune as his former Christian Anti-Jewish Party, denouncing the Holocaust as a "GIANT PROPAGANDA HOAX" and praising Adolf Hitler as "a Whiteman [who] once meted out justice to the Jews."

One day after the Temple bombing, NSRP member Kenneth Chester Griffin approached Atlanta police and made the following statement:

I was present at a meeting of the National States' Rights Party, at 524 Flat Shoals Ave., S.E., in the second week of May 1958. Also present were Billy Branham, George Bright, L.E. Rogers, and Wallace Allen.

During the course of this meeting, Wallace Allen brought up the subject of dynamiting the Jewish Synagogue on Peachtree St. He stated that J.B. Stoner could be counted on to go to Anniston, Ala. to pick up the dynamite from KKK there. And that Billy could be a watcher while Wallace was in the get away car and the two Bowling boys would plant the dynamite and one of Ace Carter's men from Birmingham, Ala. would set the fuse to it. I opposed such a move.

George Bright was to draw the diagram to place the dynamite and Wallace would case the building for the job. Wallace stated that he would be able to obtain the dynamite. And that 20 sticks should do the job. Wallace stated that J.B. Stoner could be counted on to bring the dynamite in a suitcase at night. The suitcase would be a cardboard type. He was to bring the dynamite to Wallace Allen who would then go with the other members of the party to plant and set off the dynamite.

J.B. Stoner was to leave town and go to Chattanooga while this was going on. No definite date was set for the bombing. No more was said in regards to this bombing there at subsequent meetings. We had approximately 8 meetings after this one and this bombing was not discussed with me. I believe that after I objected to the bombing I was left out of the plans....

Billy Branham stated around the first of June that it might be necessary to take drastic action in case the Henry Grady High School became integrated. During the discussion of the dynamiting of the Jewish Synagogue on

Peachtree St., it was suggested that one of the charges should be put behind a column....

At a meeting it was suggested that it was best to bring outside men to do the jobs instead of local members and to use black unknown cars as get away cars. The Nights of the White Camellia [*sic*] of Tallahassee, Fla., of which Bill Hendricks [*sic*] is affiliated, believes in using drastic means to achieve their aims....

Rogers' phone call [on October 12] was the first inkling I had that such a bombing was to occur or did occur. I had not been in contact with any of the members of the organization except Rogers and Bright. I had not phoned nor seen Wallace Allen, J.B. Stoner or the Boling [*sic*] boys during this period of time and did not know of their plans or preparations. Billy Branham had stated on more than one occasion the Bowlings were too hot to handle at regular meetings but could be counted on to do the necessary work. The implication being dynamiting.

Fulton County's grand jury indicted five suspects on October 17, under an 1897 statute that made bombing of "any dwelling house, storehouse, barn, depot, or other house or place of business or lodging" a capital crime. The defendants included Wallace Allen, Richard Bowling, brother Robert Bowling, George Bright—and informant Kenneth Griffin. Police arrested all five on October 18 and pronounced the case solved. On that same day, the Confederate Underground warned grand jury leaders:

You're going to pay for it. We're going to kill all of you who indicted those innocent men.

No attacks were forthcoming, but the prosecution had other problems. On October 29, Griffin recanted his earlier statement. Perhaps unnerved by his inclusion with the others slated for a trip to the electric chair, Griffin wrote a second statement that read, in part:

When we got to the Station, they tried to be nice and said, "Now, we just want to merely ask you a few questions and then we will turn you loose." So they proceeded to ask about the Bowling boys to which questions I said I hardly know those boys....I don't believe, however, they were mixed up in any kind of bombing, I am quite sure they aren't.

And they wanted to know about Billy Branham, and I said I had not seen Billy Branham since he left [Atlanta] shortly after the picketing [of the

Atlanta Journal in July 1958]....Then they wanted to know about Wallace Allen, and I told them I had not seen Wallace Allen in at least eight weeks and I didn't know what he was doing, but I was sure he didn't have anything to do with any bombing.

Then they wanted to know about George Bright, and I said, "George I know is not connected with anything like that."...The only thing we had talked about was mailing out some literature, we never mentioned any bombing [or] dynamite in any shape, form or fashion....

Finally they appeared to be mad and they said, well, send him on back, and they sent me on back to the fingerprinting room...and this fingerprint man was kind of a bit of smart alec and he grabbed my sore thumb and twisted it—twisted my thumb belonging to my broken arm, it ached all night long, and I was unable to get any sleep the rest of that night....

I kept repeating I wanted to see my lawyer, and all they would do would be to make a sneering remark about he [J.B. Stoner] is on the run, he can't help you, what you want to see him for, and not any other lawyer will take this case, and your only hope is just to tell us all you know. They started smearing Wallace Allen, they said that Wallace Allen was getting rich off this, I was just a sucker, and that George Bright was getting the money off of this, also....

Finally about two o'clock they said, "You haven't had anything to eat, have you?" I said no and so they said, "Why come on with us, we will get you something to eat," and so they carried me out, without having any Court Order to do so, and carried me over to Evans Restaurant on Ponce de Leon, and bought me a dinner, and they were fairly licking their chops in anticipation of the juicy information I was going to give them, and I told them that I was not, and so clammed up on them. I didn't know anything, and this made them mad and they finally took me back, got back about 2:30 to the cell. It wasn't but a little over an hour until they came again with the same old business and they—by this time—they had me practically out of my mind, constant questions to try to scare me, worrying the life out of me, and so, they set in on me again, and after about an hour or two, I decided the only thing to do was to give them a false story so that I could get out and they shut their mouths up and I might get hold of a lawyer.

I had had this wild dream one time about a bombing, and [it] is substantially the same story I told them, and [Sergeant Marion] Blackwell added a few little twists of his own on to it....They carried me off again without having any Court Order to do so, and we went over to Grant Park....

They started in on me trying to get me to say I'd testify before the Grand Jury and they'd let me off and I said "I am not going to testify against these boys because they are innocent, they are innocent, you just tricked me into signing that statement there, and it is not true and I am not having any part in any Grand Jury testimony."

Of a polygraph test that yielded inconclusive results, Griffin said, "They made it too tight around my chest purposely to where it would show up bad and then kindly [*sic*] emphasized certain questions and kept repeating the question over and over—four times and more times instead of four, and they took it, they came back in with the tale that I was lying to them and would I take the test over. I told them no, I wouldn't take the test over."

As for Griffin's prior references to Stoner, Ace Carter, and Florida Klansman Bill Hendrix, he now said, "I just created that in trying to send them off on a wild goose chase."

George Bright faced trial alone in December 1958, chosen because an October search of his home had revealed a draft of a letter threatening Atlanta Jews with "a terrifying experience." Defense counsel James Venable purged the jury pool of Jews and any person who admitted dealing with a Jewish merchant, while Judge Durwood Pye seated one prospect who admitted prior Klan membership. Another juror later told reporters, "You know, it wasn't but two hundred years ago that blacks were eating each other in the jungles of Africa."

U.S. Klans leader Eldon Edwards attended Bright's trial, assuring journalists that the indicted bombers were not Klansmen "and never will be." Asked for his opinion of the temple bombing, Edwards said, "I'm just as interested in things of this nature as the law enforcement officers themselves." The wizard failed to mention that he would be called to testify on Bright's behalf.

In place of Ken Griffin, prosecutors offered two key witnesses against Bright. The first, Leslie Rogers, was a local janitor and paid informer for the FBI inside the National States Rights Party. Derided on the stand by Venable as "a police pimp," Rogers established Bright's membership in the NSRP and sketched the group's practice of plotting violent acts

Klan attorney James Venable represented George Bright at his first bombing trial.
Credit: National Archives

against Jews. Next up was Jimmy Dave DeVore, Bright's recent cellmate in the local jail, who claimed that Bright "told me he didn't do the actual bombing, but that he rode as a lookout." Other details of the crime emerged, he said, during "numerous or several" conversations over a three-week period, each lasting "four to six hours a day."

The defense case opened with an alibi for Bright's movements in the predawn hours of October 12. His sister-in-law testified that Bright left home "sometime after midnight," while a cashier and Atlanta Patrolman Paul Green saw him in a pharmacy at 2:30 a.m. Oddly, that testimony failed to account for the time when terrorists probably planted their bomb, its timer set for detonation at 3:30. Eldon Edwards took the stand on December 6, telling jurors that "L.E. Rogers has a bad reputation. I would not believe the man under oath." U.S. Klans "klabee" (treasurer) John Felmet echoed that judgment verbatim, as did Wesley Morgan, exalted cyclops of Atlanta's N.B. Forrest klavern. Arthur Cole, an aged NSRP member from Tennessee who claimed "I've got some awful good Jewish friends," recalled meeting Rogers in August 1958, at a Kentucky gathering where Rogers asked about purchasing dynamite. George Bright closed the trial with testimony on his own behalf, denying any taint of anti-Semitism and claiming that Rogers "planned the whole Temple bombing scheme and framed me and the four other men indicted."

Jurors deliberated for eighty-four hours, then pronounced themselves hopelessly deadlocked on December 10, with nine voting for conviction and three holding out for acquittal. Judge Pye declared a mistrial, and the state prepared to try again.

Bright switched attorneys before the next trial, dismissing James Venable in favor of flamboyant Reuben Garland, Sr. On January 12, 1959, before Judge Jeptha Tanksley, Garland's opening statement branded Leslie Rogers the Temple bomber, acting "as part of a plot to collect the reward money." Renowned for his skill at rattling the strongest of witnesses, Garland cast doubt on testimony from synagogue leaders, Atlanta police, and FBI agents.

As his own key witness, Garland called Marilyn Craig, an inmate of Milledgeville State Hospital, who was granted leave to speak under a Georgia law permitting testimony from lunatics during "lucid intervals." Craig said she had known George Bright for "about two weeks, a little more" before the bombing, and she had accompanied Bright to a local pharmacy at 2:30 a.m. on October 12, 1958. Their errand: collecting supplies for an all-night vigil to glimpse the satellite *Pioneer II* as it passed over Georgia. Prosecutor Tom Luck caught her in a lie concerning when and where the satellite's launch and subsequent failure were publicized, but it made no difference. Jurors acquitted Bright on January 24, after deliberating for thirty-five minutes. Charges against the other four defendants were dismissed.

The View from Eastview

Whether or not any Alabama Klansmen played a part in the Atlanta Temple bombing, Robert Shelton had troubles enough of his own with the knights of Eastview 13. Bull Connor had done his best for white supremacy in Birmingham—ignoring fourteen cross-burnings at local schools on August 31, 1958; issuing an order twelve days later that his officers must not cooperate with federal investigators; jailing three black ministers in October 1958, when they arrived from Montgomery to plot a Birmingham bus boycott—but Dynamite Bob still nursed a grudge over his brief detention in July. Drunk as usual, Chambliss crashed a meeting of the Democratic Party's state committee at the Tutwiler Hotel, and squared off with Connor in the crowded ballroom. "You drug me out of bed at three a.m.," he raged, "and threw me in old sol [solitary confinement]. You treated me worse than a goddamned nigger. You're a nigger lover and a liar!"

Still, Chambliss was not Shelton's worst problem in Birmingham. Unknown to the grand dragon, he soon had a federal informer spying from within his ranks. Gary Thomas Rowe was a larger, louder version of Bob Chambliss, a self-proclaimed boozer, brawler, and womanizer known to friends as "Tommy." FBI files state that he was born in Savannah, Georgia, sometime during 1933, and quit school after the eighth grade. By the 1950s, he had moved to Birmingham, gaining a reputation with police for drunken fighting. His bid to join the Jefferson County Sheriff's Department failed because he lied about attending high school. Still obsessed with law enforcement, he befriended agents of the Bureau of Alcohol, Tobacco, and Firearms, reporting illegal moonshine stills in exchange for discount prices on confiscated guns. Rumors circulated that he might be posing as an agent of the FBI.

FBI informer Gary Thomas Rowe.
Credit: National Archives

Enter Barrett Kemp, recently assigned to the FBI's Birmingham field office. A background check on Rowe revealed that he had paid a $30 fine in September 1956, on a charge of impersonating a police officer. Anxious to discourage any civilian from pretending to be a G-man, Kemp visited Rowe's home to sort out the problem. Rowe denied impersonating a fed, then perked up when Kemp asked whether he knew any Klansmen. In fact, Rowe knew several from the bars he frequented, dismissing them to Kemp as "crazy" and "a bunch of assholes." Nonetheless, Rowe eagerly agreed to Kemp's suggestion that he join the Klan as an informer. "And that was how they got me," he later explained. "The FBI was God."

Discrepancies abound in the reports of Rowe's federal service. Rowe himself claimed that he first heard from Kemp "toward the end of 1959," while FBI records place the initial contact months later, on April 4, 1960. Rowe biographer Gary May writes that Rowe put out feelers "a few days later," and was soon invited to join the Alabama Knights of the KKK, led by Robert Shelton.

Despite his ties to Alabama's governor elect, Shelton had fallen out of favor with U.S. Klans leader Eldon Edwards. Alabama's secretary of state had received a letter from Edwards on November 4, 1959, ordering that Shelton's name be deleted as "authorized agent" of the U.S. Klans. No replacement was named at the time, and Edwards subsequently wrote a second letter reinstating Shelton—then reversed himself again on April 11, 1960, naming Alvin Horn as Shelton's replacement in the grand dragon's post. Shelton responded by announcing the creation of an "independent" Klan, claiming that seventy percent of U.S. Klansmen would be joining him.

The ink was barely dry on that press release when the FBI opened its file on Gary Rowe, on April 18, 1960. Another month elapsed before Shelton filed incorporation papers for his Alabama Knights of the Ku Klux Klan, on May 17. Speculation persists that Governor Patterson played some role in the rift between Shelton and Edwards, seeking to maintain relations with a homegrown Klan. In any case, Rowe's formal "naturalization" into Eastview 13 occurred on June 23, 1960. Within two months, Rowe was promoted to serve as Klokan Chief—in charge of klavern security and investigation of prospective recruits. On September 1, Rowe supervised creation of a dozen "action squads," assigned to carry out cross-burnings and other forms of harassment—directed, according to Rowe, by Sergeant Tom Cook, who had failed to entrap Jesse Stoner.

"Missionary Work"

White Birmingham faced perils aplenty from black encroachment by 1960. On February 1 of that year, the first sit-ins occurred at whites-only lunch counters in North Carolina, and the movement spread like wildfire. Alabama got its first taste of "direct action" protests on February 25, when thirty-five students from all-black Alabama State College occupied the lunchroom at Montgomery County's courthouse. Police dispersed them, but the demonstrators returned two days later, braving attacks by Klansmen armed with baseball bats that left the students bloodied. Police refused to intervene, and Governor Patterson endorsed their apathy on February 29, announcing that there were "not enough police officers" in America "to prevent riots and protect everybody" if blacks "continue to provoke whites." If protests continued in the capital, Patterson warned, "someone is likely to get killed."

Bull Connor shared that sentiment in Birmingham, announcing on February 26 that he would "not permit organized, planned, and deliberate efforts to foment violence and interfere with the rights of others." Fred Shuttlesworth coordinated the city's first student sit-ins, at five downtown department store lunch counters, on March 31. Connor's police moved swiftly, arresting the demonstrators on charges of "trespass without warning." Crowing to the press, Bull said, "That was quick, wasn't it? It looks like I've been police commissioner long enough for the Negroes to have learned that I'm not going to put up with this kind of carrying on."

While Shuttlesworth regrouped, word spread that Birmingham blacks were planning a bus boycott similar to Montgomery's. In late August, "Grand Titan" Hubert Page told members of Eastview 13 that it was time to "strike down at the niggers" who occupied white seats on city buses. Action squads armed with chains, blackjacks, and lead-weighted baseball bats were assigned to ride the buses and beat any blacks who budged from their seats at the rear. By then, Gary Rowe recalled:

> Slapping Negroes on buses was such an established habit for Klansmen that if they were asked whether anything unusual had happened that day, they would not think to mention it.

Members of the Klan's female auxiliary volunteered to ride the same buses armed with long hatpins. Robert Shelton's knights referred to such assaults as "missionary work."

By August 1960, the rival U.S. Klans was in decline. A heart attack killed Eldon Edwards in Atlanta, on August 1, and his successor as imperial wizard—Robert "Wild Bill" Davidson—inspired no confidence, particularly inasmuch as Edwards's widow backed another would-be leader, Rev. Earl George. Davidson struck a defiant pose, then abruptly resigned in February 1961, replaced by George. On February 21, four U.S. Klan defectors obtained a Georgia charter for a brand-new group, the Invisible Empire, United Klans, Knights of the Ku Klux Klan of America. Wild Bill Davidson led the new Klan until April 1, 1961, when he quit in favor of Georgia Grand Dragon Calvin Craig.

JFK vs. KKK

The Klan's internal wrangling took a backseat to presidential politics in 1960. Determined to scoop its major rivals, the National States Rights Party convened in Dayton, Ohio, on March 19, nominating Arkansas Governor Orval Faubus as its presidential candidate, with Alabama's John Crommelin as his running mate. Faubus, despite his reputation as a die-hard segregationist who pardoned convicted Klan bombers, declined the nomination, but the NSRP was deaf to his protests. Whether he liked it or not, the party was using his name.

The Democratic front-runner was John Fitzgerald Kennedy, despised by Klansmen and their allies as a liberal Massachusetts Catholic. Bigots rallied against JFK in West Virginia's primary, on May 10, cranking out reams of anti-Catholic literature, but Kennedy carried the day with timely aid from singer Frank Sinatra and infusions of cash from underworld friends of his millionaire father. Klansmen who hoped for a replay of 1924's Democratic convention got a reprise of 1928 instead, with Kennedy securing first-ballot nomination on July 13, 1960.

Republicans chose Vice President Richard Nixon as their standard-bearer two weeks later, and the candidates squared off for a series of televised debates. In their third debate, on October 13, responding to a statement from congressman Adam Clayton Powell that "all bigots will vote for Nixon," Kennedy replied:

> Mr. Griffin, I believe, who is the head of the Klan, who lives in Tampa, Florida, indicated a—in a statement, I think, two or three weeks ago that he was not going to vote for me, and that he was going to vote for Mr. Nixon. I do not suggest in any way, nor have I ever, that that indicates that Mr. Nixon has the slightest sympathy, involvement, or in any way imply any inferences in regard to the Ku Klux Klan. That's absurd. I don't suggest

that, I don't support it. I would disagree with it. Mr. Nixon knows very well that in this—in this whole matter that's been involved with the so-called religious discussion in this campaign, I've never suggested, even by the vaguest implication, that he did anything but disapprove it. And that's my view now. I disapprove of the issue. I do not suggest that Mr. Nixon does in any way.

Orval Faubus, unwilling presidential candidate of the NSRP in 1960.
Credit: Library of Congress

Nixon quickly agreed, but the damage was done. The Kluxer in question—William Griffin, Florida grand dragon of the U.S. Klans—told reporters, "I don't give a damn what Nixon said. I'm still voting for him."

Kennedy's race for the White House made unexpected waves in Alabama, where Governor Patterson and his 1958 campaign manager, Charles Meriwether, endorsed JFK. Robert Shelton shuddered at that news, warning members of his brotherhood that "Klansmen should stay away from Kennedy and keep an eye on John Patterson and Charles Meriwether. They are tools of the Jews." Soon afterward, Shelton was fired from his job at B.F. Goodrich, a hasty "reduction in force" that Shelton described as political retribution.

On election day, November 8, Alabama gave five of its electoral votes to Kennedy, while the other six went to 1940s kleagle-turned-Senator Robert Byrd (also receiving Mississippi's eight votes, plus one from Oklahoma). Arkansas, Georgia, Louisiana, both Carolinas, and Texas remained in the Democratic column, while Nixon carried Tennessee and Virginia. The votes that really mattered, though, were found in Illinois, where leaders of Chicago's Mafia would boast of putting JFK in the White House.

The NSRP scored less impressive results with its unwilling presidential candidate, but J.B. Stoner and company were still encouraged by the final tally of 214,195 votes for Faubus and Crommelin. While they failed to carry a single state, observers found it telling—and chilling—that an avowed neo-Nazi group could claim nearly a quarter-million votes from coast to coast.

Chapter 6
Freedom Riding

In January 1961, Bull Connor made his bid to hand-pick a successor for Birmingham's retiring commission president, James Morgan. His choice was Arthur Hanes, Sr., the son of a Methodist minister, born in 1916. Hanes had distinguished himself as an athlete at Birmingham–Southern College, then obtained a law degree from the University of Alabama before joining the FBI. He left the bureau in 1951 to serve as chief of security at Birmingham's Hayes Aircraft plant. From that post, possibly unknown to Connor, Hanes collaborated with the CIA in its illegal invasion of Cuba, scheduled to occur in April 1961, two weeks before Birmingham's Democratic primary. After the invasion failed, Hanes distributed CIA death benefits to the widows of pilots shot down over Cuba.

Arthur Hanes, Sr., FBI agent, Birmingham politician, attorney, and alleged Klansman.
Credit: National Archives

On racial matters, Hanes shared Connor's view of blacks and segregation—an attitude only reinforced by his years of service under FBI Director Hoover. Since the *Brown* decision, Hanes had also been a popular speaker for various racist groups, including the John Birch Society and Ace Carter's North Alabama Citizen's Council. Hanes knew Klansmen well and welcomed them as clients in his legal practice, when they were indicted. Gary Rowe reported to the FBI that Hanes joined Eastview Klavern 13 in 1961, and later wrote that the Klan "campaigned for Hanes; we put up posters, passed out literature, and took up donations." Eastview Exalted Cyclops Robert Thomas also "ordered us to attend neighborhood meetings held in high schools to promote Hanes's candidacy." Still, Hanes was outwardly respectable: his sister served as principal at Mountain Brook Elementary School, while his son, Art, Jr., was enrolled at Princeton University.

He was the best of both worlds to white Birmingham, and Bull Connor—while campaigning to keep his own job—would stop at nothing to see Hanes elected.

Primary Colors

Birmingham held its municipal Democratic primary on May 2, 1961. Connor faced three challengers for his job, while Hanes squared off against six. A landslide of ballots returned Bull to office, but Hanes trailed rival Thomas King—former aide to eleven-term Congressman George Huddleston—by 1,500 votes, forcing a runoff between the contenders on May 30.

Before the votes were even counted on May 2, Hanes and Connor hatched a plot to smear King as a "nigger-lover." On primary day, with ballots still incoming, Hanes appeared on television to observe that King had carried Birmingham's "Legion Field boxes," racist code for a black neighborhood whose residents rented their front lawns for parking during college football games at Legion Field stadium. Alarmed by that development, King bowed to advisors who urged that he court Connor's favor before the runoff.

King met Bull in Connor's office on May 9, "to pay his respects." As King later explained, "I knew there was no way that I could get him to support me, but we hoped at least to get him not to come out for my opponent." During their fifteen-minute chat, Connor "was very cordial....We shook hands, I told him I thought we could work together cooperatively, and he said he felt sure we could." As King left City Hall, he was accosted by a black stranger who called his name and thrust out his hand. King shook it and moved on, unaware that a hidden photographer had caught him in the act. Copies of the photo quickly surfaced, bearing a caption that read "Defeat the NAACP Bloc Vote." King had no doubt who was behind the fraud. "Nobody knew I was going to be at City Hall," he said, "except Commissioner Connor."

On May 29, in his last speech before the runoff, Hanes told supporters that he had Bull Connor's vote. Furthermore, he said, "You may be assured if my opponent is elected tomorrow that this will be hailed as the fall of the South's greatest segregation stronghold." King fired back, calling Hanes a "race-baiting coat-tail rider," but the damage was done. The next day, Hanes defeated King with 21,133 votes to 17,364.

Days of Rage

No impartial observer could doubt that Birmingham's racial tensions had grown more intense by 1961. Jesse Stoner and Edward Reed Fields were former Columbian members. The Columbian group was a Klan-allied neo-Natzi group active in 1946. Fields was a chiropractor who shared Stoner's obsessive hatred of Jews. Jointly, they led The National States Rights Party, and moved its headquarters to Birmingham from Louisville, Kentucky, early in the year, hoping, as Stoner wrote, to "save Alabama and the nation from Jew Communists and their nigger allies." And while the NSRP may have ranked as Birmingham's most extreme racist faction, the Ku Klux Klan was by no means idle.

Gary Rowe fed the FBI a steady stream of information from Eastview Klavern 13, involving the Klan's ongoing "missionary work"—ride-alongs with local police, assaults on buses, and at lunch counters, the chain-whipping of a man who allegedly molested his teenage stepdaughter—with those accounts including Rowe's participation in assorted violent crimes. When warned to limit his felonious involvement, Rowe advised his bureau handlers:

> Hey, you can't go out with carloads of fifteen men and say, "Hey, I'm going to stand off to the side and look at you while you beat these damn people." You either get in there or leave it alone or you're gonna get killed.

On April 6, 1961, for example, Rowe and fourteen other Klansmen were told to remain and "move some heavy equipment" after a regular klavern meeting. The phrase was code for an assignment: they were driving out to Odenville, in St. Clair County, to terrorize an elderly white couple—Orman and Pauline Forman—who cared for the "fudge ripple baby" of an single white mother and her onetime lover, an African American soldier. Plans were vague—to "beat the hell out of" the Formans, possibly to kill the child—but Pauline spoiled the fun by opening fire on the knights with a pistol. They returned fire, and while no one was hit, raider Charles Cagle ran into a boulder and broke his kneecap. The raid's planner, John Jones, was so embarrassed that he quit the Klan, and thereby missed the hooded order's greatest triumph of the year.

Conspiracy

One week after the Forman raid, on April 13, Detective W.W. "Red" Self approached Gary Rowe, saying that Sgt. Tom Cook desired a meeting to discuss matters "of interest" to the Klan. While cruising in Self's squad car, the detective told Rowe that police "needed to get ahold of some people in the Klan that can keep their god-damned mouth shut. Something big is coming to Birmingham, some freedom riders in buses. We want some people to meet them and beat the shit out of them."

Rowe met Cook at a local restaurant on April 17, receiving the names of several "inter-racial organizations," their membership lists, and the locations of upcoming civil rights meetings. At the same time, Cook warned Rowe that an unknown informer—in fact, Rowe himself—had warned the FBI of Ku Klux plans to raid Rev. Alfred Hobart's Unitarian Church, deemed a hotbed of liberal activity. A search for the spy was in progress, Cook said, with an eye toward prosecuting him on false charges. "The jury could be fixed," Cook said, "to have the individual sent to the penitentiary."

Cook met Rowe again on April 20, this time providing three police files on Rev. Martin Luther King, Jr. and the Alabama Council on Human Relations, asking Rowe to "determine whether the material therein could be printed on the Klan press and distributed to Klan members." Cook also asked the Klan to mount surveillance on the ACHR's meetings and record license numbers of visiting cars, to identify "Jews and Communists" supporting the group. As to the freedom riders, Cook told Rowe:

> I don't give a damn if you beat them, bomb them, murder or kill them. I don't give a shit. There will be absolutely no arrests. You can assure every Klansman in the country that no one will be arrested. We don't ever want to see another nigger ride off the bus into Birmingham again. I want it to be something they remember as long as they live. Now, when you get the signal from Red to get the hell out of there, leave then. We've only got about two, three minutes at the most and you'll be swarmed with officers."

Rowe returned Cook's documents to police headquarters on April 24, whereupon Cook told Rowe "that any information he had in his files would be made available to the Alabama Knights, Knights of the Ku Klux Klan, Incorporated. Informant stated at that time Cook opened two file drawers in his office and told informant to help himself to any material he thought he would need for the Klan."

On May 11, Grand Titan Hubert Page told the assembled knights of Eastview 13 that two busloads of freedom riders would reach Birmingham on Sunday, May 14—Mother's Day. Robert Creel, visiting exalted cyclops of the Bessemer klavern (later the state's grand dragon), suggested that "a few picked men" stationed along the highway "could put a few loads of buckshot" into the buses, but police had apparently backed off their approval of outright murder. Page quoted Bull Connor as telling him, "By God, if you are going to do this thing, do it right!" Specifically, any demonstrators entering the bus depot should be beaten until they looked like "a bulldog got a hold of them." Anyone trying to use the restrooms should be stripped naked and thrown outside, where police would charge them with indecent exposure. Connor guaranteed fifteen minutes of mayhem without police interference. Knights were warned to leave their Klan I.D. at home, carry only registered guns, and arm themselves with baseball bats. Aside from Eastview 13, klaverns from Bessemer, Gardendale, Helena and Warrior were on "special call" for the event.

Rowe advised his FBI contacts of the plot between police and Klansmen, but the bureau dragged its feet. It was May 12 before headquarters authorized Birmingham's top G-man, Thomas Jenkins, to advise local police that "some violence" might be impending. Jenkins was specifically barred from mentioning the Klan or freedom riders, warned from Washington that "we should be most meticulous to protect the informant and the source of information." Jenkins phoned Chief Moore, who advised that he would be out of town on Mother's Day, referring Jenkins to Sgt. Cook for any further contacts. And indeed, on May 14 Jenkins called Cook—known to Jenkins as the Klan's contact—to tell him that the buses had left Atlanta for Birmingham.

The rest is bloody history. In retrospect, Agent Jenkins excused himself on grounds that he was simply following orders. He relayed the freedom riders' travel plans to Cook—and thereby to the Klan—he said, because Cook "was the one who was supposed to be in charge of the Birmingham Police Department at that time. Who else was I going to call?"

"A Good Job"

The buses rolling toward Birmingham in May 1961 had, in a sense, been waiting to travel for seventeen years. In 1944, Virginia police jailed a Baltimore-born African American, Irene Morgan, for refusing to let a white passenger take her seat on an interstate Greyhound bus. Morgan appealed her conviction to the U.S. Supreme Court, which announced its decision in June 1946, voiding any state laws that required segregated seating on interstate buses or trains. The Congress of Racial Equality (CORE), founded in 1941, tested that ruling in April 1947, with a two-week "journey of reconciliation" through Virginia, North Carolina, Tennessee, and Kentucky, where the first "freedom riders" suffered beatings and arrests. Washington took no steps to enforce *Irene Morgan v. Commonwealth of Virginia,* and seating on interstate transport remained effectively segregated.

On December 5, 1960, the Supreme Court struck another blow against white supremacy, in the case of *Boynton vs. Virginia,* banning segregated depots for interstate buses. Once again, the white South prepared to do nothing. And once again, CORE prepared to offer its members as human sacrifices to the cause. Movement leaders announced that a bus would leave Washington, D.C., on May 4, 1961, bearing "freedom riders" through Dixie with various stops on their way to New Orleans, Louisiana. That April announcement prompted Birmingham police to join in their criminal conspiracy with Klansmen, while the FBI preserved its policy of observation and inaction.

The riders left as scheduled on May 4, logging their first arrest in Charlotte, North Carolina, four days later. The first individual assault occurred on May 9, in a depot at Rock Hill, South Carolina. Two more riders were jailed on May 10, in Winnsboro, South Carolina, for trying to enter a "white" depot restaurant. By the time they reached Atlanta on May 11, the party had gained more participants and added a second bus—one Greyhound, one Trailways—for the trip to Alabama. Sgt. Cook drove to Georgia that day, observing the demonstrators and phoning their itinerary back to Birmingham for the benefit of Klansmen.

On the morning of May 14, Edward Fields of the NSRP phoned CBS News reporter Howard K. Smith to report some imminent "action" at Birmingham's Greyhound depot. Before the riders reached the Magic City, though, they had to pass by Anniston, in Calhoun County, home of a Ku Klux klavern led by former Ace Carter disciple Kenneth Adams. The Greyhound bus stopped there for sandwiches, and was immediately swarmed by Klansmen who hammered its sides with clubs and chains while shouting, "Sieg heil!" One stabbed at the tires with a knife while three local policemen watched idly from the sidelines, then cleared a lane for the damaged bus to depart.

Fifty cars filled with Klansmen followed the bus out of town, until its punctured tires went flat and forced it to a halt near Bynum, southwest of Anniston. Someone hurled a flaming Molotov cocktail through one of the bus windows, others holding its doors shut while the mob cried, "Roast 'em!" Unknown to the terrorists, two undercover Alabama Highway Patrol officers—Eli Cowling and Harry Sims—had boarded the bus in Atlanta, acting on orders from Governor Patterson. Cowling carried a hidden recording device to capture any inflammatory statements, but the threat of real flames prompted him to draw his gun and force the bus doors open, driving Klansmen back with shots fired in the air. Other state patrolmen finally arrived to lift the siege, though some sat laughing in their cars and one later gave a Klansman's confiscated bludgeon to his young son as a souvenir of the occasion.

A "freedom bus" burns near Bynum, Alabama, outside Anniston.
Credit: Library of Congress

Two freedom riders after their beating by Klansmen.
Credit: Library of Congress

The Trailways bus came next, bearing among its passengers James Peck, a 46-year-old participant in the original 1947 freedom rides, and Dr. Walter Bergman, 61, a former Michigan State University professor. As before, Klansman were waiting in Anniston, ignored by police as several boarded the bus, assaulted its passengers, then ordered the driver to proceed toward Birmingham.

There, Gary Rowe and his fellow knights stood ready at the Greyhound depot. Press reports claimed forty or fifty white men awaited the bus, while Rowe pegged the count at a thousand or more, loitering in or around the bus station. Ed Fields and Jesse Stoner were also present, though members of Shelton's Klan angrily warned them to leave. News from Anniston of the Greyhound's destruction left the keyed-up terrorists deflated, at loose ends, until police arrived to tell them that a second bus was headed for the Trailways depot. Rowe later said that Klansmen caught without a means of rapid transportation were ferried to the second target in police cars, after which the officers withdrew and vanished from the scene.

Gary Rowe (second from right, in front) joins fellow Klansmen in beating freedom riders.
Credit: National Archives

What followed was a gruesome riot, caught on camera by journalists who found themselves fair prey to Klan assaults, along with freedom riders and unlucky African American pedestrians in the vicinity. As promised by Bull Connor, no police were present while the Klansmen beat and kicked their victims senseless. Dr. Bergman was among the worst injured, suffering a stroke that would confine him to a wheelchair for the rest of his life. Howard K. Smith, forewarned, reported to the world that Klansmen:

> grabbed the passengers into alleys and corridors, pounding them with pipes, with key rings and with fists....Police did not appear until around ten minutes later, when the hoodlums had got into waiting cars and moved down the street...where I watched some of them discussing their achievements.... That took place under Police Commissioner Connor's window.

Questioned about the scarcity of his patrolmen, Connor told reporters that his force was understaffed on Sunday, since so many of his officers had stayed at home for Mother's Day. No Klansmen were arrested, and Detective Self congratulated the rioters, saying, "Y'all did a good job. Now why don't you go on home and get a good night's sleep."

As luck would have it, Gary Rowe and several others still had too much nervous energy. They went in search of other victims, attacking several black men then met along Tenth Avenue. Unwilling to be pummeled, one of the men pulled a knife and slashed Rowe's throat, causing Rowe to fear that he was dying. Klansman Billy Holt drove Rowe to the home of a Klan-friendly doctor, who sutured his wound and pronounced it minor. Next morning, the *Birmingham News* ran a front-page photo of Rowe and others beating one of the freedom riders, but Rowe's back was turned to the camera, and gullible FBI agents accepted his lie that the burly thug was someone else entirely. Rowe received an extra $175 on top of his normal $90 weekly salary, for his "material assistance" to the bureau, with a notation that "he was seriously injured in performance of his duties for the FBI."

More Rides, More Riots

On Monday, May 15, the battered Birmingham riders prepared to face another mob scene in Montgomery, their next stop on the freedom trail. Governor Patterson officially withdrew protection, telling journalists:

> The citizens of the state are so enraged, that I cannot guarantee protection for this bunch of rabble-rousers.

In case state troopers missed the point, Patterson warned that any officer who cooperated with the FBI on civil rights investigations would be fired immediately. Fearing more damage to company property, Greyhound canceled its afternoon bus to Montgomery, over protests from U.S. Attorney General Robert Kennedy. By then, another mob of Klansmen ringed Birmingham's Greyhound depot, held at bay by Connor's police and their dogs until the demonstrators agreed to leave town. They boarded a plane to Montgomery, delayed in turn by a Ku Klux bomb threat.

Conditions were no better in the state capital, where another mob of whites attacked and beat more freedom riders aboard a bus arriving from Birmingham on May 20. Police Commissioner L.P. Sullivan watched from his cruiser nearby, telling reporters:

> We have no intention of standing guard for a bunch of troublemakers coming into our city.

Ten minutes later, when the mob had grown from 200 to 1,000 or more, Alabama Public Safety Director Floyd Mann risked his life and his job to rescue a TV newsman and an unconscious black victim at gunpoint. Local police and sheriff's deputies finally arrived to disperse the mob an hour and fifteen minutes after the riot began. One mob victim, federal observer John Siegenthaler, lay unconscious on the pavement as Commissioner Sullivan stood nearby. When asked to call an ambulance for Siegenthaler, Sullivan replied, "He has not requested one."

In Washington, Robert Kennedy ran out of patience, dispatching U.S. Marshals to Montgomery on May 21, where yet another howling mob besieged Dr. Martin Luther King and some 1,500 African Americans inside a local church. Governor Patterson, formerly supportive of the Kennedy "New Frontier" as long as it left southern blacks to their fate, reluctantly declared martial law in Montgomery, dispatching National Guardsmen who escorted the captive parishioners home on May 22.

Freedom rides continued, winding their way through Mississippi to Louisiana, facing more arrests and violence along the way. The riders were victorious at last: On September 22, 1961, the Interstate Commerce Commission issued orders formally banning segregation aboard interstate buses or within their terminals after November 1. Even then, however, white resistance continued. On April 9, 1962, a policeman in Taylorsville, Mississippi, beat and fatally shot black army corporal Roman Ducksworth Jr., aboard a bus from Maryland. Local authorities deemed the killing "justifiable homicide."

As for the Alabama Klan, federal agents arrested nine Anniston members on May 22, charged with fire-bombing the Greyhound eight days earlier. Prosecutors dropped charges against two defendants on January 16, 1962, while six more faced trial the same day. All six were convicted, five sentenced to probation after promising to sever all connections to the KKK. The sixth defendant, received a sentence of 366 days in jail, to be served concurrently with time imposed for a separate burglary conviction. The ninth defendant was acquitted by another jury.

Forced to act by media photos showing the faces of grinning rioters, Birmingham police finally arrested three Klansmen from Tarrant County—Jesse Thomas Faggard, son Jesse Oliver Faggard, and John Hampton Thompson—who paid $30 fines and served thirty days in jail on misdemeanor charges of disorderly conduct. The nearest thing to punishment for Klansmen or police in Birmingham and Montgomery was a federal lawsuit. At trial before Judge Frank Johnson in Montgomery, various lawmen were excused on the basis of conflicting evidence and testimony. Robert Shelton, Alvin Horn, and their respective Klans escaped with an injunction banning any future interference with "peaceful interstate travel by bus."

New Klans, New Victims

Agent Barrett Kemp submitted his resignation from the FBI six days after the Birmingham riots, retiring to private practice of law. Informed of Kemp's decision, Gary Rowe threatened to quit the Klan as well, but Kemp prevailed over him by convincing him to remain in place despite his contempt for his new handler, Agent Charles Stanberry, whom

Rowe described as "dumb" and "senile," prone to attending risky public meetings where his standard-issue G-man garb "stood out like a sore thumb." Still, Rowe was addicted to the cloak-and-dagger games, the federal drinking money he received, and the opportunities for violent action.

And change was in the wind for the Invisible Empire. On July 8, 1961, Robert Shelton met with Calvin Craig of the new United Klans and members of several smaller Klan factions at Indian Springs, Georgia. Together, they created a new, improved United Klans of America with Shelton installed as imperial wizard and Craig as his Georgia grand dragon. Over the next four years, the UKA would claim klaverns in nineteen states, ruled from Shelton's headquarters in Tuscaloosa. Despite its solid base, Alabama—with forty klaverns—still lagged behind North Carolina (192), Mississippi (76), Georgia (57), and South Carolina (with 50). Shelton, although a committed racist, also shared the vision of 1920s Klan leaders who viewed the order as a cash cow. He soon created a front group, the Alabama Rescue Service, which banked a portion of each member's monthly dues for Shelton's personal use. In 1965, congressional investigators noted that, while Shelton claimed total income from all sources as $18,487.60, his hidden earnings from the KKK exceeded $100,000 ($703,000 today).

In Birmingham and environs, there was no shortage of "missionary work" after the freedom rides. Two incidents from December 1961 are typical. The first involved a nightclub called The Barn, where rumor had it that black musicians sometimes danced with white waitresses. Knights from Eastview 13 and Bessemer's "Young Men's Social Club" turned out with shotguns and leaded baseball bats, planning to "burn The Barn and get rid of it" in Rowe's words, but they called off the raid upon finding the bar too crowded. Days later, five black customers turned up at the Krystal Kitchen, a diner favored by Klansmen in North Birmingham. Rowe and two fellow knights were present when the blacks arrived, assaulting them with brass knuckles, dragging one man outside and hurling him into the path of oncoming traffic.

Police arrived in the midst of the mini-riot, seizing Klan weapons, arresting Rowe and his cohorts on charges of assault with intent to commit murder. On arrival at the Southside City Jail, prisoner Earl "Shorty" Thompson identified himself and the others as Klansmen, whereupon the booking sergeant said, "Take your weapons and go home. You've done enough good for one night." Rowe claimed that officers also invited one Klansman, Gary Gregory, to have sex with an intoxicated female prisoner in their custody, as a reward for having "done a good job that night." Rowe reported the fight and arrests to Agent McFall, whose memo to headquarters omitted any mention of Rowe's participation.

Holding the Color Line

While Klansmen thus amused themselves, Birmingham faced a new challenge to segregation. In December 1961, a federal court ordered full integration of sixty-seven local parks, thirty-eight playgrounds, eight swimming pools, and four golf courses by January 15, 1962. Commission president Hanes, unwilling to submit, closed the facilities, slashed $295,000 from the city's park budget, and fired all those employed at the affected sites.

That draconian move raised some hackles in white Birmingham. The *Post-Herald,* no slouch at defending apartheid, raised the editorial question, "Why not keep the parks open and give our people a chance to see whether they can continue to operate without trouble?" Concerned white citizens raised the same question a week before Christmas, at the next city council meeting, but Hanes would not be moved. "You for opening the parks?" he asked the audience. "Then, friend, you're for integration. You for closing them down? Vice versa. It's as simple as that."

A delegate from the Jefferson County Women's Service Legion gave Hanes the benefit of the doubt, saying, "You're realistic, Commission President, and you must know that integration is coming ultimately whether we like it or not." Hanes snapped back, "That's your opinion madam. I don't think any of you want a nigger commission president or a nigger police chief. But I tell you, that's what'll happen if we play dead on this park integration."

The Klan, of course, agreed wholeheartedly. On the night of January 16—one day after integration would have proceeded without Hanes's interference, the same day Klansmen faced trial for burning the freedom ride Greyhound—bombs exploded at three of Birmingham's black churches: New Bethel Baptist, the Temple Church and Kingdom of God and Christ, and St. Luke's AME Zion. The blasts caused minimal damage, and no injuries. Local papers noted that none of the targets was linked to civil rights "agitation," but Bull Connor staunchly insisted, "We know Negroes did it." His proof: two patrolmen sitting in their car seventy-five yards from the scene of one blast reported a black teenager running nearby.

Gary Rowe phoned Agent McFall at 12:20 a.m. on January 17, two hours and twenty minutes after the third blast, to report the bombings. Rowe thought some Eastview knights might be responsible, suggesting Bobby Frank Cherry as a prime suspect. For his own part, Rowe advanced an alibi, claiming that he and Klansman Harry Walker had gone to "visit" an interracial couple for some "head-knocking," but their intended victims were not at home. McFall later denied any suspicion of Rowe's involvement in the blasts, saying that he was "proud of [Rowe] for being on the ball."

April 1962 brought more excitement for the Klan, as nearby Bessemer prepared to celebrate its Diamond Jubilee with a public fair. After one night of festivities, Eastview's knights received alarming reports of blacks boarding various carnival rides and shopping at booths on the midway, "mixing with and molesting white people." Accordingly, a "select group" of Klansmen from Eastview and four other klaverns assembled—with Gary Rowe among them—to patrol the carnival, armed with chains hidden in popcorn boxes. Rowe later claimed that he accidentally dropped his chain in front of a policeman who picked it up, returned it, and told him, "If you're going to have a show, why don't you get it started? We're cold standing here."

The resultant "show" consisted of a bloody brawl between Klansmen and fifteen to twenty blacks, with some whites also punching one another. Later asked how many people he had beaten, Rowe replied, "I don't know how many people. A hell of a bunch of them." Rowe also claimed that he delivered a full report of the riot to Agent McFall—who, in turn, said that he had no memory of the event or Rowe's participation in the violence.

The Klan's next scheme, hatched in July, was a plot to kill Fred Shuttlesworth. Harlan Hobart Grooms, the same federal judge who had ordered Autherine Lucy's admission to the University of Alabama, now demanded integration of the Dobbs House Restaurant at Birmingham's airport. Shuttlesworth, despite a recent move to Ohio, planned to be among its first black diners, and rumors quickly spread that two white women from Detroit would join his group to "hold hands with some of the Negroes." On July 19, Hubert Page passed Eastview Klansmen a message from Sgt. Tom Cook. Bull Connor and Commission President Hanes reportedly claimed that they were "tired of the way things are going in the racial situation in Birmingham but that their hands were tied." City Hall wanted the Klan to intervene by killing Shuttlesworth when he invaded the restaurant on July 21 or 22.

As with the freedom rides, Page said police had offered their cooperation in the murder plot. They would disarm Shuttlesworth's bodyguards, then one of the cops would fake a heart attack as a distraction while Klansmen mobbed the black party and one of them—John "Nigger" Hall, nicknamed for his dark complexion—would fatally stab Shuttlesworth. Rowe later claimed that he objected to the plan, saying that Shuttleworth's death would "only cause more trouble," but his komrades were "too worked up to listen to reason." Page promised that Governor Patterson would pardon Shuttlesworth's slayers, even if they were sentenced to die.

Rowe informed Agent McFall of the conspiracy, and for once FBI headquarters authorized intervention. Agents warned Shuttlesworth on July 20, and he postponed his Alabama visit. When Rowe and others reached the Dobbs House on July 21, they found a swarm of police protecting a small contingent of black customers. The dine-in passed without incident. On August 5, Agent McFall filed a report lauding Rowe as "without doubt, the most alert, intelligent, productive, and reliable informant on Klan and racial matters currently being operated by the Birmingham office."

Friends in High Places

If Robert Shelton had fallen from favor with Governor Patterson, he soon found a new patron and friend in George Wallace. Running hard for governor in 1962, Wallace recruited Shelton and his knights to help him keep his promise that he would not be "out-niggered" again. Not satisfied with one Klan leader in his camp, however, Wallace also put Ace Carter on his payroll.

The full extent of Wallace's involvement with Carter remains controversial. In 2001, after both men had died, author Allen Barra wrote:

> Till the day he died, George Wallace denied that he ever knew Asa Carter. He may have been telling the truth. "Ace," as he was called by the staff, was paid off indirectly by Wallace cronies, and the only record that he ever wrote for Wallace was the word of former Wallace campaign officials such as finance manager Seymore Trammell."

Meanwhile, journalist Robert Sherill, writing in 1968, named Carter as "[o]ne of Wallace's closest cronies and advisors." Klan historian David Chalmers says that Wallace personally commissioned Ace to write his 1963 inauguration speech.

Of course, the "fightin' little judge" from Barbour County had to get elected first. He faced seven opponents in the Democratic primary, including then-Lieutenant Governor Albert Boutwell, Attorney General MacDonald Gallion, ex-governor Jim Folsom, Tuscaloosa attorney Ryan DeGraffenried, Sr., ex-state senator J. Bruce Henderson, Wayne Jennings—and Bull Connor.

Sadly for Bull, Wallace already had the Klan vote in his pocket. Robert Sherill found Wizard Shelton "on the most intimate terms" with Wallace in 1962, providing knights to nail up campaign posters and harass competitors as they had done for Patterson in '58. Bob Chambliss was among the eager volunteers, telling cronies that Wallace had promised Klansmen an all-expenses-paid fishing trip to the Gulf of Mexico if he won the election. Eastview 13 supplied a panel truck to carry Wallace literature side-by-side with copies of the NSRP's *Thunderbolt* newspaper—financed, it was said, with $7,500 from Wallace campaign headquarters.

Another campaign aide was ex-highway patrolman Albert J. Lingo, known for being "hell on niggers." Lingo served as Wallace's personal pilot during the gubernatorial race, with side trips to sit on the dais at KKK rallies, where he was introduced as "a good friend of ours." Slated to replace Floyd Mann as chief of the state police when Wallace occupied the governor's mansion, Lingo served as liaison with volatile racists.

In his public speeches, Wallace definitely sounded like a Klansman. He branded federal judge Frank Johnson of Montgomery "a low-down, carpet-baggin', scalawagin', race-mixin' liar," and promised cheering crows that:

> I shall refuse to abide by any illegal federal court order, even to the point
> of standing in the schoolhouse door in person.

On May 1 primary voters cast 207,062 for Wallace, 160,704 for DeGraffenried, and 159,640 for Folsom. The other five contenders split 109,867 ballots. Bull Connor ran fifth in the field, with 23,019, while Lt. Gov. Boutwell polled a humiliating 862. (John Crommelin, mounting his fifth Senate race in twelve years, was crushed by four-term incumbent Joseph Lister Hill, but consoled himself with 11.5 percent of the vote.)

Wallace continued rigorous campaigning through the runoff on May 29, when he beat DeGraffenried by a margin of 340,730 to 269,122. Republicans offered no gubernatorial candidate for the general election on November 6, and independent rival Frank Walls of Tuscaloosa offered no real competition, his 11,789 ballots swamped by a Wallace landslide of 303,987.

Preparing to keep his campaign promise of a stand "in the schoolhouse door," Wallace sent Al Lingo off to Oxford, Mississippi, to observe the riots that accompanied integration of that state's university in September 1962. Robert Shelton followed Lingo, with a small planeload of ranking knights, but local air traffic controllers refused him permission to land.

Minor embarrassments aside, the KKK was ecstatic over Wallace's election. Bull Connor had less reason to celebrate in November, after local Citizens for Progress secured 11,000 signatures on a petition seeking to change Birmingham's form of government, adopting a mayor-council system. Bull fought the move, rhetorically asking the Chamber of Commerce:

> Do you burn down your barn if there are rats in it? If you don't like what I am doing, impeach me, but don't change your form of government.

On November 6, voters picked change over the status quo, by a margin of 18,068 ballots to 16,415. Connor struck a philosophical pose, telling reporters:

> I have but one thing to say. The people have voted, and if they want a council, that's democracy.

But he was not prepared to leave without a fight.

At 9:15 p.m. on December 14, 1962, a bomb shattered windows at Bethel Baptist Church, injuring two children who were wrapping Christmas presents in the basement, blacking out the Collegeville neighborhood when it downed power lines. Bull Connor visited the scene, telling reporters the bombers "ought to be hung when they're caught," but he soon reverted to his standard line: "We know the Negroes did it." City spokesmen announced a $1,000 reward for capture of the bombers on December 17, increased to $3,000 the following day. Robert Shelton chimed in on Christmas Day, pledging $1,000 to the cause, but his knights had nothing to fear. Connor's cops would make no arrests.

Segregationists protest James Meredith's admission to the University of Mississippi in September 1962.
Credit: Library of Congress

Chapter 7
"Segregation Forever"

On New Year's Day 1963, Klansman Tommy Blanton drove a girlfriend through Fountain Heights, looking for trouble. He spotted a black pedestrian crossing the street in front of him and gunned his car forward, swerving toward the human target. His intended victim dodged in time, leaving Blanton to tell his frightened date that he had wanted "to kill the black bastard."

Ten days later and a few blocks from the site of the aborted hit-and-run, black bail bondsman Maurice Ryles found a scorched paper bag outside his home. In the bag were four sticks of dynamite, their fuse burned down to a dud blasting cap. Ryles had no part in the civil rights movement as yet, but would soon, when a new campaign dubbed "Project X" brought marchers to the streets of Birmingham.

A Klan-ridden Society

Native writer William Bradford Huie—author of best-sellers, including *The Revolt of Mamie Stover* (1951), *The Execution of Private Slovik* (1954), and *The Americanization of Emily* (1959)—described Alabama under Governor George Wallace as "a Klan-ridden society," wherein the hooded order was encouraged by officials to ignore and violate prevailing law. Examples of that infestation were not difficult to find.

At his inauguration on January 14, Wallace delivered a fiery speech penned for the occasion by Ace Carter, ending with the declaration:

> In the name of the greatest people that have ever trod this earth, I draw the line in the dust and toss the gauntlet before the feet of tyranny. And I say, Segregation now! Segregation tomorrow! Segregation forever!

As noted by Diane McWhorter, the final phrases were lifted directly from Ku Klux fliers of the 1920s that read, "Here Yesterday! Here Tomorrow! Here Forever!"

More than words alone marked Wallace's connections to the Klan. Among those that were publicized:

Al Lingo, the Klan's "good friend," took command of the state highway patrol and renamed its patrolmen "state troopers," decorating their cars and uniforms with Confederate flags.

Wallace forced a highway construction firm to hire Robert Shelton as a "public relations consultant" at $4,000 per year ($29,000 today), a post retained until the U.S. Bureau of Public Roads complained in 1964.

When Wallace created an Alabama Legislative Commission to Preserve the Peace, probing "communist" influence over the civil rights movement, he chose Ralph Roton—a tenth-grade dropout who served as head of the UKA's "Klan Bureau of Investigation"—as its chief investigator.

The American Southern Publishing Company, hired to print all state textbooks, also publishes Shelton's newsletter, the *Fiery Cross,* along with UKA pamphlets and membership cards.

Nor were the governor's favors to the Klan simply political payback. As soon as Wallace appointed new members to the state parole board, in July 1963, that panel reversed its 1960 ruling that Edward Aaron's mutilators must serve at least one third of their twenty-year terms, amounting to a minimum of six years and six months each. Over strident protests from their prosecutor, Jesse Mabry was released in February 1964, Bart Floyd in January 1965, Grover McCullough and Joe Pritchett before year's end. During that same busy year, Wallace supporters in the state legislature defeated a bill designed to keep dynamite from the hands of bombers.

Raging Bull

Bull Connor, meanwhile, was engaged in the second-worst political fight of his life. An associate of Bull's filed an appeal against the November vote approving Birmingham's new mayor-council government, but Connor hedged his bets by running for mayor under the revised system. Armed with announcements that the next mayor would earn $10,000 more per year than outgoing Commission President Art Hanes, Connor told voters, "I'm running for the $15,000 job of mayor, not the $25,000 job. I'll never approve such a change unless they let the people vote on it." If that appeal failed, Bull trumpeted his plan to save Birmingham "from the Washington blight."

On March 5, voters cast 17,437 ballots for mayoral candidate Albert Boutwell against 13,778 for Connor, while perennial candidate Tom King claimed 11,639. Working up to the runoff on April 2, Connor told supporters that he had quit the local Chamber of Commerce "because they tried to brainwash Ol' Bull about integration."

On March 8, right-wing preacher Billy James Hargis brought his Christian Crusade to Birmingham for a presentation dubbed "Operation Midnight." Sharing the dais with Hargis was ex-general Edwin Walker, ringleader of the 1962 segregationist riots at the University of Mississippi. In the audience, Eastview Klansmen rubbed shoulders with Dr. Ed Fields and Ace Carter, while Robert Chambliss manned the door as an official greeter, handing out Connor campaign pamphlets.

Documents in Connor's FBI file suggest that he considered a plan to arrest the bombers of Bethel Baptist Church on election eve, but he could not bring himself to do it. In the runoff vote, Boutwell defeated Connor by a tally of 29,630 to 21,648. The people had spoken *again*, but Bull was disinclined to listen. Despite a headline in the *News*, proclaiming that a "New Day Dawns for Birmingham," Connor was not going anywhere just yet. Officially retaining office until April 15, Bull and his bookends—Hanes and Commissioner James "Jabbo" Walker—insisted that their terms would only end as scheduled from their last election, on October 1, 1965. Birmingham would meet its next crisis with two mayors in place, while Bull Connor commanded the police and fire departments.

Project X

As America's "most segregated" city, Birmingham was a natural target for civil rights protests. "Project X" was conceived in the latter part of 1962, after Dr. King's Southern Leadership Conference (SCLC) conducted a disappointing campaign in Albany, Georgia. There, Police Chief Laurie Pritchett defused demonstrations by using nonviolent methods, but his sage advice to do likewise in Birmingham fell on deaf ears with Bull Connor.

Project X was a combined effort of King's SCLC (represented in Alabama by younger brother Rev. A.D. King of Birmingham), Montgomery's Rev. Ralph Abernathy, and Fred Shuttlesworth's ACMHR. Demonstrations were scheduled to begin on March 14, 1963, with Connor forewarned by spokesmen for the ACMHR. "You will not get a permit to picket in Birmingham, Alabama," Bull told his visitors. "I'll picket you over to the jail." Movement leaders martialed their forces, postponing their initial protests until early April, while Connor consulted the Klan. His message, delivered by homicide detective Maurice House, was succinct: Police alone would deal with demonstrators. "We want to keep our friendship with the Klan," House said, "but if you try to help us you will be arrested."

Unknown to Connor's cops, and perhaps to Robert Shelton, frustrated knights from Eastview 13 began meeting with NSRP leaders Jesse Stoner and Edward Fields. Gary Rowe reported the meetings to his FBI handler. On March 24, bombers struck at another black home, wounding two occupants. Police blamed unknown blacks for the blast, deeming it "non-racial," but the FBI knew better. Rowe had notified Agent McFall of the explosion shortly after it occurred, although he named no suspects.

Demonstrations began in Birmingham on April 2 and continued through May 10. Bull Connor was no Laurie Pritchett, as he quickly proved by fielding attack dogs and high-pressure fire hoses against protesters of all ages. Images from the embattled city flashed worldwide on television, raising widespread outcries against police brutality. Abernathy and the King brothers were among hundreds arrested.

Local Klansmen, sidelined from the festivities, occupied themselves in other ways. The UKA created a new political front group, United Americans for Conservative Government, which welcomed members of the NSRP, the Citizens' Councils, and the John Birch Society. Frustrated members of Eastview 13 formed a new secret circle, the Cahaba Boys, named for their meeting place near the Cahaba River. Tommy Blanton vandalized the car of a Catholic neighbor on Easter Sunday, April 14, then accidentally shot one of his fellow Klansmen that night, while modifying a pistol. (The wounded knight lost a kidney.) Three days earlier, the *Birmingham News* had offered $87,125 for information leading to conviction of local bombers, whom it branded "WANTED For the Attempted Assassination of Birmingham, Alabama." As usual, the notice brought no takers.

Birmingham police field attack dogs against peaceful demonstrators, April 1963.
Credit: Library of Congress

"Mississippi or Bust"

In the midst of Birmingham's turmoil, a white postal worker and CORE member, William Lewis Moore, launched a one-man "freedom walk" from Chattanooga, Tennessee to Jackson, Mississippi. For the occasion, Moore wore a sandwich sign reading "Equality for All—Mississippi or Bust."

Moore hoped to stop along the way, in Birmingham, to spend time with his aunt and uncle, Charles and Helen Cagle. When contacted, they discouraged him from visiting their home. Presumably unknown to Moore, Charles Arnie Cagle was an active member of Eastview Klavern 13, suspected of bombings and known to be one of the freedom ride rioters.

On April 23 Moore was shot and killed on a highway near Attalla, Alabama. Police traced the .22-caliber murder weapon to owner Floyd Simpson, a white grocer from Collbran, in DeKalb County, who held the rank of "klokan" (investigator) in the UKA's Fort Payne klavern. Simpson was jailed on April 25, though accounts differ as to whether he was charged with Moore's slaying or simply held as a material witness. In either case, he was never prosecuted. FBI agents questioned Simpson two years later, regarding

Klansman Floyd Simpson (center), flanked by attorneys William Beck and Roy McCord, faced no charges in the death of William Moore, murdered with Simpson's rifle. *Credit: Library of Congress*

possible involvement in bombings around Birmingham, but again no charges were filed. Author Mary Stanton reports that Simpson quit the Klan in 1968. Moore's death remains officially unsolved.

Surrender and Reaction

On May 10, leaders of the Birmingham movement negotiated limited desegregation plans with members of a Senior Citizen's Committee, chaired by longtime racist organizer Sidney Smyers. Bull Connor condemned the settlement on May 11, calling for a boycott of stores that planned to integrate. That night, the United Klans rallied knights from six states at a site midway between Birmingham and Bessemer.

Before blazing crosses, Robert Shelton read a list of shopkeepers who had capitulated, noting that "most of them were Jews or foreigners." He praised Connor's efforts, adding that "Klansmen would be willing to give their lives if necessary to preserve segregation in Alabama."

The rally broke up at 10 p.m. Forty-five minutes later, two bombs exploded at the home and parsonage of A.D. King. Shortly before midnight, another bomb struck the A.G. Gaston Motel, which served as SCLC headquarters for the Birmingham campaign. That blast injured four persons, while causing extensive damage to the motel and three nearby house trailers. Hundreds of angry blacks poured into the streets, stoning police and setting fire to several stores. Al Lingo cordoned off a twenty-eight-block area with 250 state troopers, augmented by local police and 100 "irregulars"—many of them suspected Klansmen—led by Dallas County Sheriff Jim Clark, visiting from Selma. Dozens of blacks were beaten, some forced into the homes of strangers as police cleared the streets. Miraculously, no one was killed.

Bomb damage at the A.G. Gaston Motel.
Credit: Library of Congress

Gary Rowe contacted Agent McFall with the riot still in progress, claiming an informant in the black community had blamed the bombings on unidentified Black Muslims. McFall was skeptical, and while Eastview's best-known bombers all had suspiciously airtight alibis, Diane McWhorter calls the May bombings "the best planned Klan action" since 1961's bus station riots.

There was a glitch, however. Black laborer Roosevelt Tatum had witnessed the bombing of A.D. King's home, informing FBI agents that the charges were delivered by a uniformed policeman driving Car 22. Rather than investigate Tatum's story, G-men charged him with making false statements to federal agents. U.S. Attorney Macon Weaver convened a federal grand jury on June 28—a month ahead of its normal schedule—to investigate Tatum. Although ordered by superiors in Washington to drop the case, Weaver forged ahead and secured an indictment on August 26. Convicted at trial on November 18, Tatum received a one-year prison term. The driver of Car 22, though easily identified, was never questioned.

On May 15, Art Hanes addressed 1,000 members of the Klan's UACG at Birmingham's Municipal Auditorium, raging against the "Congolese mob" of protesters, branding Dr. King a "witch doctor," and excoriating members of the Senior Citizens Committee as "weak-kneed quisling traitors." Hanes assured his cheering audience that he would "never negotiate or meet with the communists or the rabble rousers of the King type because they haven't got anything to negotiate with. They haven't got a thing that we want. We have what they want."

But not for long. On May 23, the Alabama Supreme Court upheld Birmingham's new mayor-council form of government. Hanes departed into private legal practice, where violent Klansmen would rank among his most prominent clients. Bull Connor, leaving his office with tears in his eyes, told a small group of supporters, "This is the worst day of my life."

The Schoolhouse Door

Alabama's civil rights action shifted to Tuscaloosa in June, as Governor Wallace braced himself to resist court-ordered integration of the state university. From his headquarters near campus, Robert Shelton warned that desegregation of 'Bama would "touch off the bloodiest rioting ever seen in the United States." His knights would "match the violence" of U.S. marshals or federal troops, Shelton said, and if local police failed to maintain segregation, "the Klan will enforce it."

Those words rattled Wallace, who viewed resistance "in the schoolhouse door" as his personal media moment. On June 5, six days before the university's scheduled desegregation, Gary Rowe reported that Al Lingo had ordered all Klansmen to stay clear of the campus or face arrest. Ace Carter interrupted writing of the governor's public statement to phone Edward Fields in Birmingham, at NSRP headquarters. As Fields recalled the conversation, Carter "requested that we not go down to Tuscaloosa and hold any type of demonstration. He said that it would be best for us to leave the entire event up to the governor." Bull Connor echoed that sentiment on June 7, pleading with the Tuscaloosa County Citizens' Council to "let Governor Wallace and law enforcement agencies handle the problem." It was, Bull said, "a personal request from the governor."

Predictably, some members of Eastview 13 refused to stay home. Gary Rowe and five others set off for Tuscaloosa on June 8, in two cars loaded with weapons including guns, swords, bayonets and clubs. State troopers stopped them on Highway 11 outside town, seizing the arsenal, while Rowe claimed the officers shared some confiscated whiskey with the Klansmen, one trooper remarking:

> Jesus Christ, we sure hate to bust you when you came down here to help us keep the goddamn niggers away from the school.

Nor were they "busted," strictly speaking. Instead of taking the six to jail, troopers drove them onto the university campus, where state investigator Ben Allen questioned them for several hours, then released them without filing charges. The confiscated weapons wound up at Tuscaloosa's courthouse, where Rowe and the others retrieved them on June 9. Arriving in the midst of a party for a newly elected prosecutor, the Eastview knights were treated to champagne by a judge who told them, "I want to thank you men. You're outstanding American citizens. I wish we had 10,000 more like you guys."

The brief detention caused Rowe and his friends to miss a rally of 3,000 Klansmen outside Tuscaloosa, after sundown on June 8, where Georgia Grand Dragon Calvin Craig stood before a sixty-foot fiery cross to thank God "for the greatest man in Alabama, Governor George C. Wallace."

Wallace had his moment in the spotlight at high noon on June 11, reading a brief statement penned by Ace Carter, then yielding in the face of U.S. marshals and federalized National Guardsmen. No riot ensued, and calm prevailed on campus until November 16, when a bomb exploded near the dormitory housing black co-ed Vivian Malone. Another blast rocked the campus on November 17, two more on November 21. Five National Guardsmen were charged with setting the bombs on December 22, prompting their commander to call it "a juvenile plot to have the detachment continued on duty" beyond its scheduled demobilization.

Cahaba Boys

There was nothing juvenile about the newest clique of Klansmen in Birmingham, drawn from the ranks of Eastview 13. Robert Chambliss was their most experienced bomber, joined in his contempt for Eastview's less violent "assholes" by Troy Ingram, John "Nigger" Hall, Ross Keith, Charles Cagle, Bobby Cherry, George Pickel, Herman Cash and brother William (known as "Jack"), elderly Thomas "Pop" Blanton and son Tommy, Jr. The younger Blanton's FBI file noted "a history of psychopathic behavior" and dubbed him "a degenerate of the worst sort."

Gary Rowe knew all of the Cahaba Boys, though he denied joining their breakaway klavern. In fact, he told Agent McFall that Eastview's klokan chief, Earl Thompson, had ordered Rowe and others to find the Cahaba crew's meeting place on August 15, 1963. After several drunken hours searching up and down the riverside, Rowe led the team to Troy Ingram's house, snatched him at gunpoint, and questioned him for two hours. During that time, Ingram proclaimed his loyalty to Shelton's UKA and fingered Bob Chambliss as the man responsible for "any wrongdoing."

Klan unity was critical that summer, after a July ruling from the U.S. Court of Appeals for the Fifth Circuit ordered Birmingham to desegregate its schools when they reopened on September 3. Close behind that order, on July 23, came an announcement from Birmingham's new city council repealing segregation ordinances for restaurants and other places of public accommodation as of July 30.

The impending crisis prompted a rapprochement between the UKA and the brown-shirted NSRP, with Robert Shelton admitting "there is not too much difference in philosophy" between the two groups. Jesse Stoner had been welcomed as a speaker at the Klan's Tuscaloosa rally on June 8, and his storm troopers were about to receive a stamp of official approval. Following a late-July rally near Anniston, a plainclothes state trooper drove Edward Fields and associate James Warner to meet Al Lingo at a nearby motel. As Fields recalled the meeting, "Colonel Lingo told me that if we waged a boisterous campaign against the integration of the schools and petitioned the governor for the closing of such schools and held demonstrations in front of those schools on opening day, that this would give Governor Wallace reason enough to close mixed schools." Fields agreed to help the governor in any way he could.

Bob Chambliss volunteered to circulate the NSRP petitions, while knights still loyal to Eastview 13 grew increasingly radical. At a klavern meeting on August 1, ex-convict Ronnie Tidwell offered a lesson on bomb-making. A week later he instructed Klansmen in the two-bomb technique, using a small charge to draw police and spectators within range of a larger bomb, loaded with deadly shrapnel.

Gary Rowe claimed that his FBI handlers "went completely ape" on hearing his report of the August 1 meeting. The next week, Rowe said that he interrupted Tidwell's lesson to discuss the problem of controlling local terrorism. According to his report, Rowe warned of "a power structure [*sic*] going between" the UKA and the NSRP, asserting that "[t]he States Righters will go out and pull a bunch of bullshit when we isn't prepared for it and it will fall back on us and we will catch hell and go to prison for something they did."

Birmingham heated up on August 9, as the Klan and the NSRP held separate rallies in town. Art Hanes and Bull Connor graced the UKA meeting as guest speakers, but soon lost control of their audience, Connor wading in to stop a pair of Klansmen from assaulting journalists. The following night, while Gary Rowe and thirty-odd fellow knights caused a diversionary disturbance in Warrior, straddling the Jefferson-Blount County line, Charles Cagle and prison guard Levi Yarbrough firebombed nearby St. James Methodist Church. An earlier generation of Klansmen had torched St. James in 1926, and Cagle had failed at his first arson attempt in November 1962, when the fuse on his Molotov cocktail burned out. This time—again—the church was destroyed.

On August 12, NSRP member Albert DeShazo warned his landlady to avoid Birmingham's newly integrated stores on Thursday or Friday—August 14 and 15—or she "might get hurt." On the 15th, a man resembling DeShazo set off a tear-gas grenade in Loveman's department store downtown. He evaded police and was never identified, leaving Mayor Boutwell to brand him "a human being so totally indifferent to innocent human lives."

On the night of August 20, a bomb exploded at the home of Arthur Shores, collapsing the lawyer's two-car garage. Black neighbors lobbed bricks at police and firefighters, until officers firing submachine guns dispersed them. Gary Rowe's follow-up report named the bombers as Ross Keith and Arthur White (known as "Sister" because he was "a little on the feminine side"), with Charles Cagle and John Hall serving as lookouts. Keith had nearly been deafened by the bomb's premature explosion, Rowe said, seeking emergency medical aid overnight. As usual, police made no arrests.

The stage was being set for tragedy.

Chapter 8
Bloody Sunday

All of Birmingham was apprehensive as the clock ran down to September 3 and the first day of school integration. On August 29, Jefferson County Sheriff Melvin Bailey summoned 200 local ministers—all but five of them white—to the Municipal Auditorium, where he warned them to "start preaching reconciliation." Moved by rumors that he planned to deputize the clergymen, the Klan's UACG wired Governor Wallace in Montgomery, requesting state troopers to "relieve the incompetent deputized preachers that they may revert to their pulpits and the Lord's work." In fact, there was no plan to deputize the ministers, and Wallace had already ordered Al Lingo's men to Birmingham.

School Daze

On August 31, the National States Rights Party staged a procession through Montgomery with seventy-five cars sporting Confederate flags. Edward Fields led the parade to the governor's mansion, bearing a petition signed by 30,000 racists who opposed school integration. Governor Wallace was absent, but he left a hand-written apology with Colonel Lingo, who greeted the neo-Nazis and made them feel at home. Back in Birmingham, by nightfall, Fields and Jesse Stoner addressed a rally in Cahaba Heights, accompanied by Georgia synagogue-bombing defendant George Bright.

That same afternoon, Cahaba Klansman Ross Keith had visited Robert Chambliss at home, bringing girlfriend Lavelle Fike along for the ride. At one point, Fike excused herself to use the bathroom and opened a bedroom door by mistake. On the floor before her lay four or five bundles of "giant firecrackers" tied up with twine.

On September 1, the NSRP held its annual convention at Birmingham's Redmont Hotel, observed by at least one police informant who recorded Dr. Fields's rant against Jews who allegedly controlled the Kennedy administration and the FBI. Bob Chambliss spent the afternoon helping a crippled niece and her diabetic husband—Eastview Klansman Harry Eugene Walker—move into their new home in Trussville, northwest of Birmingham. In an unusual display of generosity, Chambliss had secured the loan for their down payment on the house.

Shortly after midnight, walking his beat downtown, black Civil Defense captain James Lay saw a black 1956 or '57 Ford Tudor sedan parked beside a basement entrance to the Sixteenth Street Baptist Church, a rallying point for the spring demonstrations. A white man occupied the driver's seat; another stood beside the car, holding a satchel. They fled at sight of Lay, and while he tried to spot the car's license number, the plate had been removed. (Later, FBI agents learned that Harry Walker owned such a car. A photo array of known Klansmen revealed that the Sixteenth Street prowlers strongly resembled Bob Chambliss and Tommy Blanton, Jr.)

James Lay alerted police at 12:40 a.m. Officers L.R. Cockrum and R.F. Reese soon arrived, but their response was peculiar. According to Lay, they told him:

> You didn't hear a fucking thing. Get back up to [Arthur] Shores's house. We ought to kill you, nigger!

Neither patrolman filed a report of the incident.

On Labor Day, September 2, Governor Wallace addressed a crowd of some 10,000 segregationists at Birmingham's Ensley Park. Police detective Marcus Jones found the park "full of Klansmen" and spotted Bull Connor on the sidelines, huddled in conversation with Ed Fields and other NSRP leaders. Wallace described the recent SCLC march on Washington, D.C. as "planned and led by communists and atheists," like those—he said—who made up the bulk of President Kennedy's administration. The mob cheered Wallace's announcement that Al Lingo and 450 troopers stood prepared to guard West End High School against the enrollment of two black students. If that failed, Wallace said, he had "other secrets for Birmingham and other places" on tap.

Huddled with Mayor Boutwell after the rally, Wallace asked Boutwell to delay school openings "on the grounds that violence might erupt." Regardless of how many black children enrolled, said Wallace, "it inflames me." When he warned again of mayhem, Boutwell said, "I hope and pray there will not be." Prayers notwithstanding, Wallace answered, "What about dynamiting, blowing up?" There was a precedent for bombing, Wallace cautioned, claiming to fear that those responsible—"Negroes or maybe communists"—would strike again.

In fact, the governor, acting through Al Lingo, had ensured that there *would* be violence on opening day. September 3 found 150 NSRP members shouting, "Hang Albert Boutwell!" as they rushed police lines, hurling bricks and swinging signs on wooden stakes. Police struck back with their batons, repelling the attackers and arresting several.

Klansman Tommy Blanton joined an NSRP march on West End High, where police arrested *Thunderbolt* associate editor James Warner, but administrators stole the mob's thunder by postponing integration for two days. Rushing off to Ramsay High School, the brown-shirts fought another skirmish with police that landed four more of their members in jail. Observing Blanton's agitated homecoming that afternoon, one of his neighbors told another, "Tonight there will probably be a bombing."

Prelude to Tragedy

On September 4, 1963, Bob Chambliss bought a case of dynamite—140 sticks—with blasting caps and fuse from Leon Negron's General Store in Daisey City, near Adamsville in Jefferson County. Surmising his plan, Negron told Chambliss, "If you are going to blow up some niggers, I'll throw in a few extra sticks." That evening, Chambliss showed the explosives to other Klansmen at Jack Cash's Café, where they discussed planting a charge at the home of Arthur Shores. After midnight, FBI agents saw and photographed Chambliss, John Hall, and Charles Cagle at Bob's home, shifting the TNT from his car to Hall's. Hall and Cagle drove it to a field near Gardendale, concealed it under kudzu vines, and later told Klansman Levi Yarbrough where to find it, he then retrieving the stash for Troy Ingram.

Meanwhile, at 9:40 p.m., a bomb *did* explode at Shores's house, collapsing its façade. The first of many officers responding to the scene, Patrolman Floyd Garrett, was a nephew of Dynamite Bob. Surrounded by furious neighbors, he called for backup. Rioting spread for blocks in all directions, as more police arrived and started firing in the air or into homes. Among the wounded, one bystander—John Coley—died from a shotgun blast while standing near Floyd Garrett. Garrett denied having a shotgun at the time, contradicted by multiple witnesses, while other police falsely claimed that Coley had "burst from a house firing a gun."

Neighbors observe the home of Arthur Shores, bombed on September 5, 1963.
Credit: Library of Congress

Gary Rowe, by his own account, was in the thick of the action, personally shooting a "great big ass black man" with his .38 revolver. A police sergeant stopped him nearby, concerned that neighbors might have seen Rowe's license plate. Assured that they had not, the cop told Rowe, "Get the hell out of here, okay? Good shooting!" Agent McFall, on hearing Rowe's report, allegedly investigated and confirmed that Rowe's victim was dead—though in fact, John Coley remained the riot's only official fatality. McFall concealed the incident from headquarters, telling Rowe, "Just sit tight and don't say anything about it."

Governor Wallace responded to news of the riot on September 5, telling a *New York Times* reporter:

> What this country needs is a few first-class funerals, and some political funerals, too.

His disdain for rioters did not extend to neo-Nazis, though. Concerning the NSRP, he declared:

> It takes courage to stand up to tear gas and bayonets.

Two days later, at Birmingham's Redmont Hotel, Wallace addressed a fundraiser for the Klan's UACG. Prominent among the 489 attendees were Robert Shelton, Edward Fields, Troy Ingram, Bob Chambliss, Robert Thomas, and Gary Rowe. Wallace caused momentary consternation by pausing to hug a black waiter he knew from his hometown in Barbour County, but all was forgiven as he took the stage to blame "nigras" for dynamiting their own homes in Bombingham.

That same night, Rowe and company planned an assault on hotelier A.G. Gaston's rural home, locally known as The Castle. Approaching the house through a pouring rain, the knights lobbed two bombs—a dub that fizzled out on impact with an outer wall, and one that smashed a window, setting fire to drapes, the carpet, and a lamp shade. As they fled, future grand dragon Robert Creel affixed a sticker to the house, reading "The KKK Is Watching You." Rowe claimed that he gave Agent McFall a full report of the incident, but if so, it somehow vanished from his file.

On Sunday, September 8, the Sixteenth Street Baptist Church received two anonymous bomb threats. Later that afternoon, perhaps belatedly embarrassed by his frolic with the Klan on Saturday, Governor Wallace taped a televised call for "law and order," adding an assurance to "all the citizens of this state, both white and Negro, that my fight is not against anyone...and I have never made a single reference or statement in public in my life that reflected upon any man because of who he happened to be." At dawn the next morning, Wallace followed that lie with an order forbidding school integration.

On September 11, Cahaba Boys Bob Chambliss and Troy Ingram visited the Eastview klavern to present a seminar on bomb-making. Gary Rowe, also present, failed to notify Agent McFall. At the same time, an FBI informer in Mobile informed his handlers that "a secret meeting" had convened in Birmingham, including rabid anti-Semites John Crommelin, William Potter Gale (founder of the violent California Rangers and the Posse Comitatus movement), Noah Jefferson Carden, and "independent" Klansman Sidney Barnes, said to be in Birmingham with "several others" to murder Dr. Martin Luther King. Barnes refused to discuss the meeting with agents, and later rebuffed advances from congressional investigators.

On September 13, a diner in Jack Cash's restaurant observed Cash making a phone call. Investigators later identified the number Cash dialed as FA2-9481, belonging to a Birmingham service station where

Baggett Transfer trucks hauling dynamite routinely parked. Cash asked the other party if he had "the case," then, after apparently receiving an affirmative reply, ordered that it be taken to "the church"—a common code name for a Ku Klux klavern—in Powderly, a Birmingham suburb.

On Saturday, September 14, Elizabeth Hood visited her uncle and aunt, Robert and Flora Chambliss, at their home. Dynamite Bob, in his cups as usual, proclaimed that he had been "fighting a one-man war since 1942" against the "goddamn niggers," boasting that he had "enough stuff put away to flatten half of Birmingham." When Hood asked him what good that would do, Chambliss answered, "You just wait till after Sunday morning. They will beg us to let them segregate."

Massacre of Innocents

At 1:30 a.m. on Sunday, September 15, Birmingham's Holiday Inn received a telephone bomb threat. The hotel stood six blocks away from the Sixteenth Street Baptist Church, a target of surveillance by local police and sheriff's deputies. Instead of sending a routine patrol to investigate the threat, headquarters diverted its "special" officers from the church, leaving it unguarded for a critical two-hour period until the threat was deemed a false alarm.

At 2 a.m., black pedestrian Kirthus Glenn saw a late model white-and-turquoise Chevrolet parked a block from the Baptist church, its dome light revealing three white men inside. Later, from photographs shown to her by FBI agents, Glenn identified one of the men as Bob Chambliss.

Bomb damage to the Sixteenth Street Baptist Church, September 15, 1963.
Credit: Library of Congress

Police remove a victim's body from the Sixteenth Street Baptist Church.
Credit: Library of Congress

Cars outside the Sixteenth Street Baptist Church, damaged by bomb shrapnel.
Credit: Library of Congress

At 10:15 a.m. that Sunday, with Bible classes underway, five young girls gathered in the basement of Sixteenth Street Baptist. They included sisters Addie Mae and Sarah Jean Collins, Denise McNair, Carole Robinson, and Cynthia Wesley. They were discussing a special youth service, scheduled to begin at eleven o'clock, when a bomb exploded in the alleyway outside, at 10:22. Flying debris killed McNair, Robinson, Wesley, and Addie Collins. Sarah Collins, partly shielded by a partition, lost one eye in the blast but would survive, requiring extensive plastic surgery.

As in the wake of other recent bombings, more violence followed, exacerbated by racist groups and the tactics of white police. While sheriff's deputies successfully diverted one thousand-car segregationist motorcade bound from suburban Midfield to downtown Birmingham, other gatherings of bigots fanned the flames of black outrage. Teenagers Michael Farley and Larry Joe Sims, a teenage Eagle Scout, assuaged their frustration at missing the Midfield parade with a visit to NSRP headquarters. There, they bought a Confederate flag, then went cruising through the downtown riot zone on a motorcycle, armed with a .22-caliber pistol. Along the way, Sims shot and killed a black thirteen-year-old bicyclist, Virgil Lamar Ware.

Bloody Sunday's last fatality occurred shortly after 4 p.m., as another racist convoy cruised the blocks around Sixteenth Street Baptist, waving rebel flags and blaring horns to celebrate the bombing. Furious blacks lobbed stones at the cars, and police opened fire with shotguns, killing sixteen-year-old Johnny Robinson with a blast of buckshot in the back.

The *New York Times* described the church bombing as Birmingham's twenty-first since 1955. It was the first so far resulting in fatalities, and the age of its victims evoked outrage worldwide. Still, some—like Klan evangelist Charles "Connie" Lynch, a longtime ally of Jesse Stoner— applauded the slaying of four "little niggers" and crowed that "we're all better off." Others, including Georgia Senator Richard Russell, thought "that the Negroes might have perpetrated this incident in order to keep emotions at a fever pitch." Russell urged FBI headquarters to probe "all angles" of the case, resisting any pressure to "suppress evidence" of black guilt for political motives.

Russell had nothing to fear on that score. In fact, Hoover's agents *would* suppress critical evidence, but not in defense of mythical black bombers.

Manhunt

Despite its history of overlooking racist violence, the FBI could not ignore the Klan's latest atrocity. As Assistant Director Alan Belmont noted:

> It is one thing to explode dynamite outside a house or in an empty building, with the aim of scaring Negroes and integrationists, but it is quite another thing to take the lives of innocent children."

Headquarters labeled the case "BAPBOMB"—for "Baptist bombing"—and ultimately assigned 253 agents, led by Agent Roy Moore from Little Rock, Arkansas, to identify the perpetrators. Under pressure from the White House, Director Hoover later claimed that every possible technique was used, ranging from "constant harassment" of Klansmen to the planting of seventeen "bugs" to collect information. In public, Hoover declared that the manhunt for Birmingham's bombers were the bureau's most intense effort since 1934, when it pursued bank-robber John Dillinger.

None of it helped. Hoover's personal racism, combined with a commitment to intelligence gathering over prosecution and obsessive fear of "embarrassment," frustrated G-men in the field. Hoover specifically ordered his men to share no "blow-by-blow account" of their investigation with superiors from the Justice Department, for fear of media leaks. Headquarters also suppressed reports from informers naming FBI spy Gary Rowe as one of three Klan officers empowered to veto proposed acts of violence. In fact, some Birmingham police considered Rowe a prime suspect in the bombing, but they contented themselves with grilling Sixteenth Street Baptist's black custodian.

September 17 was a hectic day in Birmingham. Gary Rowe visited Eastview Exalted Cyclops Robert Thomas, who denied any knowledge of the bombing in his wife's presence, then took Rowe aside to admit that "the shit hit the fan," urging Rowe to "just play it cool." When Agent McFall asked for names of potential suspects, Rowe listed Charles Cagle, John Hall, Bill Holt, Ross Keith, Earl Thompson, and Arthur White, all avid participants in "missionary work." Agents questioned Hall, later reporting that results of his polygraph test suggested involvement in the bombing—but that did not stop the bureau from hiring Hall as an informer, two months later.

Also on September 17, federal judge Clarence Allgood convened a grand jury to investigate Sunday's "blackening sin against humanity."

Specifically, he ordered the panel to indict anyone and everyone involved in obstruction of his August order desegregating Alabama's schools. The *Birmingham News* rightly noted that Governor Wallace and Al Lingo should head the list of defendants, but they were in no danger. The grand jury's final bill of indictment singled out leaders of the National States Rights Party, while absolving officials who conspired with them to foil integration.

Eastview Klavern 13 held its regular Thursday meeting on September 20, with renegade Bob Chambliss in attendance. He would later claim that Gary Rowe spoke up, complaining that "we" should have "put out enough [TNT] out there to level the damn thing." At 11 p.m., a dynamite charge exploded in the yard of black North Side resident Mose Leonard, Jr., a few blocks from Chambliss's home and across the street from an all-white school. Leonard called FBI agents, who collected fragments from the bomb and advised Leonard's family to find other lodgings. A neighbor phoned local police, who drove him to a nearby field, beat him, then jailed him for public intoxication.

The following day, Elizabeth Hood visited her aunt and uncle once again. She later described Bob Chambliss watching television coverage of the bombing investigation, speaking aloud as if to the newscaster. "It wasn't meant to hurt anybody," he said. "It didn't go off when it was supposed to." Another witness, Mary Cunningham, told FBI agents a contradictory story. According to her, Hubert Page complained of the bomb's faulty timing, to which Chambliss allegedly replied, "*I* meant for it to kill someone."

Funeral service for the church bombing victims.
Credit: Library of Congress

On September 22, while police victim John Coley was laid to rest, Klansmen rallied at Birmingham's airport, staging a send-off for Eastview wife Mary Lou Holt and other UACG spokesmen on their way to Washington, bearing segregationist petitions for Alabama senator John Sparkman and Burke Marshall, head of the Justice Department's Civil Rights Division. After that rally, the Cahaba Boys convened at the Cahaba River bridge for a huddle later described by journalist George McMillan as a "kiss-of-death" meeting to protect themselves from prosecution.

Diane McWhorter names those present for the meeting as Bob Chambliss, Pop and Tommy Blanton, Troy Ingram, Hubert Page, Pershing Mayfield, Bob Gafford, UACG president Bill Morgan, and convicted bigamist Billy Lavon Jackson. According to McMillan's report, published by the *Saturday Evening Post* in June 1964, the meeting's unnamed leader declared:

> If any one of you ever talks, it will be the kiss of death for you. We join hands here and now in swearing that each of us takes a vow to kill the man who gives anything away to the police."

Despite McWhorter's listing of those present, McMillan identified the FBI's prime suspect as a crippled Georgia resident, unnamed in print but recognizable to anyone conversant with the racist underground as Jesse Stoner.

"Made to Kill"

On Monday, September 23, Atlanta police phoned Detective Marcus Jones in Birmingham, alerting him that Jesse Stoner was enroute to Alabama with NSRP members George and Albert Bright. Jones and other officers tailed the trio to party headquarters but observed no suspicious activity. Wiretaps on the NSRP office captured furious complaints of FBI harassment, but revealed no incriminating information.

At 12:15 a.m. on September 25, a Catholic priest returning from Huntsville saw a car resembling Tommy Blanton's Chevrolet, with two male occupants, turning off Second Street toward a black neighborhood on Birmingham's south side. At 1:31, a bomb exploded in that district, eighteen blocks south of the Chevrolet sighting. Gary Rowe called Agent McFall from a phone booth three minutes later, reporting that he "just happened" to be in the area and had heard the blast. Patrolmen Jimmy Vines and J.D. Allred, responding to the blast, saw Rowe at the phone booth and stopped to speak with him, accepting his claim that: "I don't know nothing."

Proceeding to the blast site, Vines and Allred were present with other investigators when a second bomb detonated, fifteen minutes after the first. This one, loaded with nails and scrap metal, damaged eight homes and four parked cars. Inspector J.W. Haley told reporters that "this was a booby trap...made to kill."

Gary Rowe called the FBI's field office again at 3:12 a.m., learning from the dispatcher that Patrolmen Vines and Allred wished to see him again. He went to meet them at a local restaurant, but left when he found them having breakfast with a sergeant Rowe did not recognize. Later in the week, Rowe said, Vines and Allred confronted him, complaining that they did not care how many "niggers" Klansmen killed, but shrapnel bombs might also kill police. Meanwhile, UKA investigator Don Luna named Rowe and a friend, Patrolman Lavaughn Coleman, as the actual bombers. Ignoring that claim, G-men reported that Rowe was "doing a good job" in keeping track of Klan violence.

Busted

George Wallace felt the heat from BAPBOMB but refused to shoulder any of the blame, despite his call for "first-rate funerals" and his ongoing friendship with the Klan. By late September it was clear that officers would find no blacks to frame for any of the recent bombings. The next best solution, for all concerned, was to lay the blame squarely on dissident Cahaba Boys—as long as none served any major time.

On September 28, state police captain R.W. Godwin drove Hubert Page to Huntsville for a polygraph exam. Questions posed to him included knowledge of the bombing, the names of those responsible (specifically including Chambliss), and personal assistance in construction of the bomb. Page's response to each question revealed "definite" and "extreme" deception. Polygrapher Lee Greene declared that Page "definitely has knowledge of the bombings, Arthur Shores' residence, Sixteenth Street Church, and the [shrapnel] bombing at Center Street South. He is lying about his participation in these bombings and definitely attended the Cahaba ["kiss-of-death"] Meeting. The man is a fanatic." Despite those findings, no charges were filed.

On the same day, FBI agents questioned Bob Chambliss, recording details of his long Ku Klux career and his denials of specific crimes. They might have been surprised to hear their prime informer, Gary Rowe, discuss the BAPBOMB case that night, while drinking with Detective Red Self at the local VFW hall. "I'll tell you one thing," Rowe confided. "They will never solve the Sixteenth Street bombing because me and another guy did it."

On September 29, another secret meeting convened in Birmingham, at the St. Francis Motel. Present for the state police were Al Lingo and Major William Jones. Ex-mayor Art Hanes attended, with UACG attorney Wade Wallace (a distant cousin of the governor) and UACG president Bill Morgan. Klansmen in attendance included Robert Shelton, Don Luna from the KBI, Herbert Reeves (a suspect in the second Shores bombing), Robert Thomas, and prime bombing suspect Hubert Page. While no minutes of that meeting have survived, it bore immediate results. At 8:30 p.m., the governor's office announced that an arrest in the church bombing case was "imminent," expected to occur "within a few hours."

Even as Wallace's spokesman alerted the press, state police fanned out to collect five suspects for questioning. Those lifted from home included Bob Chambliss, Charles Cagle, John Hall, Ross Keith, and Levi Yarbrough. Klansman Don Luna accompanied the officers dispatched to grab Dynamite Bob. Still, despite the governor's announcement—and the bomber's defection from Eastview 13—Robert Shelton told Chambliss "not to worry, the Klan would take care of him."

And such, in fact, turned out to be the case. Chambliss, Cagle, and Hall were slapped with a misdemeanor charge of illegally possessing dynamite, on evidence so flimsy that no officer would sign the formal paperwork. (Al Lingo finally signed it himself.) All three were convicted in City Recorder's Court on October 9, fined $100, and sentenced to 180 days in jail, then were released on bond pending appeal. George Wallace crowed that "We certainly beat the Kennedy crowd to the punch," but it was all a sham. An appellate court overturned all three convictions in June 1964, and the charges were dismissed.

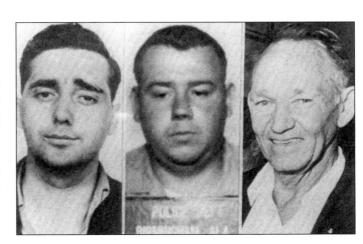

Klansmen John Hall, Charles Cagle, and Robert Chambliss (left to right), jailed on misdemeanor charges in October 1963.
Credit: National Archives

Chapter 9
"Open Season"

By the time Governor Wallace and Al Lingo performed their charade with Klansmen Chambliss, Cagle, and Hall, Dr. King and his SCLC had chosen Selma, seventy miles south of Birmingham, as the next Alabama battleground. The birthplace of Bull Connor, Selma was also the site of the Civil War's last major battle, fought one week before General Lee's surrender, with future Klan wizard Nathan Bedford Forrest leading Confederate forces. The city's Edmund Pettus Bridge was named for a Reconstruction-era Klansman and later U.S. Senator Edmund Winston Pettus. Curiously, Selma had no klavern of its own during the 1960s, but it had Klansmen aplenty. They were fond of drinking at the Silver Moon Café, and in their semi-sober moments, many rode with Dallas County Sheriff Jim Clark's "special posse."

On October 15, 1963, Dr. King visited Selma to coordinate the first phase of an intense voter-registration campaign. Sheriff Clark, wearing a "Never" button on his uniform, stood ready to oppose black registrants with any means at his disposal, backed by Lingo's troopers and a pool of vigilantes who were glad to make the hour's drive from Birmingham.

Sheriff Jim Clark (with club) harasses African Americans seeking to register as voters.
Credit: Library of Congress

In fact, black Justice Department attorney Thelton Henderson reported that a carload of white "rosin chewers" had followed his car that very day, October 15, when he loaned it to Dr. King for the trip to Selma.

FBI vs. KKK

On October 19, at a ballpark in Gardendale, Jesse Stoner convened a "White Rally" where King, Fred Shuttlesworth, and President Kennedy were hanged in effigy. Stoner regaled the audience of 150, including Bob Chambliss, with fanciful tales of Jews controlling the FBI. Chambliss, for his part, told Detective Marcus Jones that he was "having sport" with agents sent to follow him, turning the tables when he could, to trail their cars through Birmingham.

On October 22, agents in Detroit showed photos of Tommy Blanton's car to Sixteenth Street witness Kirthus Glenn, who deemed it identical to the Chevrolet she saw on September 15. Two days later, shown photographs of twenty BAPBOMB suspects, Glenn picked a mug shot of Bob Chambliss, but left his two companions from the bombing unidentified. Bureau headquarters decreed that the evidence was insufficient for indictment.

Between the FBI's visits to Glenn, on October 23, Governor Wallace announced plans to empanel a special grand jury—not to investigate bombings, but rather to probe allegations that police had photographed DOJ attorney Thelton Henderson's car, enabling Klansmen to trail him—or it—wherever the vehicle went. In Wallace's view, Henderson and his employers had "impugned the honesty and integrity of state and county law officials." Said officials, in fact, had no good reputation to preserve, and nothing came of the investigation beyond Wallace claiming that "big black Justice Department limousines" ferried civil rights activists around his state.

Meanwhile, on October 29, Klansman John Hall joined the motley ranks of FBI paid informers, pledging his best efforts to solve the BAPBOMB case. His recruitment was peculiar, since he should have been a prime suspect. A September polygraph test revealed that Hall had "some knowledge of the bombing of Sixteenth Street Baptist and may have participated in some way in the bombing or the planning thereof." The Birmingham field office warned headquarters that Hall "undoubtedly participated in some of Birmingham's minor bombings." As likely suspects in the case, Hall named Bob Chambliss, Troy Ingram, and Tommy Blanton.

By November 1963, the United Klans of America faced new competition next door, in Georgia. E.E. George, a former leader of the U.S. Klans, chartered a new Improved Order of the U.S. Klans that month, based at his home in Livonia, expanding to claim five klaverns in Alabama and Florida. Meanwhile, longtime Klansman and lawyer James Venable left his post as the UKA's imperial klonsel to lead his own National Knights of the KKK, chartered in association with William Hugh Morris and Hebert Wallace "Wally" Butterworth, a Pennsylvania native who had teamed with Venable in 1962 to found the Defensive Legion of Registered Americans. Over the next two years, the National Knights claimed four Georgia klaverns, three in Louisiana, three in Ohio, with one each in Alabama and North Carolina. Its "Black Shirt" unit ranked among the South's most violent action squads.

On November 22, three weeks after Venable founded his Klan, America was shaken by the news of President Kennedy's murder in Dallas, Texas. Conditioned by nonstop racist propaganda, Birmingham high school students cheered the announcement of Kennedy's death, adding a jibe at their mayor with the chant "Eight, six, four, two, Albert Boutwell is a Jew!"

"Somebody of Major Importance"

Agent McFall retired from the FBI in January 1964, after introducing Gary Rowe to his new handler, Agent Brooke Blake from the BAPBOMB investigative team. Blake considered Rowe "somebody of major importance to the government," but also recognized him as "a tough character" and "the type who would run off and put his safety in jeopardy if you didn't dominate him." Rowe, in turn, admired Blake as "a formidable fighter...not a man to take any guff from the Klan."

In Washington, J. Edgar Hoover had vetoed plans to charge Bob Chambliss with the Sixteenth Street bombing, filing a memo that declared any hope of conviction "remote." Nonetheless, he ordered Birmingham's field office to ensure that the case "receive continuous aggressive action and that all investigative avenues be pursued in an effort to obtain sufficient evidence so that successful prosecution can be secured."

Those efforts included planting an illegal bug in Tommy Blanton's apartment, which captured on tape an argument between the Klansman and his wife. Jean Blanton asked if Tommy had broken a date with her on Friday night, September 14, to see another woman. Tommy denied it, saying that he had attended a Klan meeting under the Cahaba River bridge, for the purpose of "planning the bombing." Another tape, made while Blanton rode in the bugged automobile of Ku Klux informer Mitchell Burns, revealed Blanton saying:

> They ain't gonna catch me when I bomb my next church. The boys done a good job on this one. There are a few Negroes now who won't grow up to bother us.

Those were confessions of a sort, but the apartment bug was illegal, its evidence inadmissible in court, and Blanton's reference to "the boys" identified no one. Hoover's order against prosecution remained firmly in place.

"Stand Up For America"

On July 2, 1964, President Lyndon Johnson signed a new civil rights act banning discrimination based on race, color, religion, or national origin in hotels, motels, restaurants, theaters, and all other public accommodations engaged in interstate commerce. By that time, Governor Wallace had already tossed his hat into the ring as a contender for the Democratic presidential nomination, running on the slogan "Stand Up For America" (retooled from 1962's motto, "Stand Up For Alabama").

Granted, the Democrats already had a man in the White House, but "accidental president" LBJ required a legitimate win at the polls to make his title stick for four more years. Governor John Reynolds entered Wisconsin's April primary as Johnson's surrogate, predicting that even 100,000 votes for rival Wallace would be a "catastrophe." When the votes were counted on April 7, however, Wallace claimed 266,000 ballots out of 780,000 votes cast, jeering at Reynolds that "there must have been three catastrophes in Wisconsin."

Cartoonist Herblock lampoons George Wallace's association with the KKK in 1964.
Credit: Library of Congress

President Johnson chose to use another surrogate, Governor Matthew Welsh, for Indiana's primary, running on the slogan, "Clear the way for LBJ, vote Welsh the fifth of May." Wallace, recognizing Indiana as a stronghold of the 1920s Klan, denounced "sweeping federal encroachment" against states' rights, while touring with a Catholic bishop in support of a constitutional amendment allowing state-sponsored prayers in public schools. Wallace lost that race, but still polled 31 percent of the Democratic vote, 172,646 ballots out of 376,023 cast.

Maryland was Wallace's last hurrah on the primary circuit, and his best showing yet. Governor John Millard Tawes declined to serve as LBJ's surrogate, leaving the chore to Senator Daniel Brewster. Recent ghetto riots in Cambridge were a symptom of the Old Line State's racial division, and Wallace made the most of it. On May 19, while Brewster emerged victorious, Wallace claimed 47 percent of 500,000 ballots cast.

While it was clear that Wallace would not be his party's presidential candidate, his racist base remained hopeful. In Alabama, the UKA's United Americans for Conservative Government distributed 500,000 sample ballots bearing Wallace's name—and "accidentally" omitting that of congressman Carl Atwood Elliott, a relative liberal (by Ku Klux standards) who consequently lost his House seat in the primary runoff election.

While Klansmen, including Bob Chambliss, flocked to Wallace in 1964, the National States Rights Party was divided. In Maryland's primary, its spokesmen hailed Wallace as the "last chance for the white voter," but in fact the NSRP had already nominated its own candidate two months earlier, choosing ex-convict John Kasper as its presidential standard bearer, backed by running mate Jesse Stoner. Diehard optimist John Crommelin challenged incumbent George Grant for his seat in Congress, losing the May 5 primary with 21,469 votes to Grant's 47,656.

On July 4, 1964, Wallace traveled to Atlanta for a "Patriot's Rally Against Tyranny," held at Lakewood Park. Accompanied by a contingent of United Klansmen that included Gary Rowe, Wallace shared the stage with Georgia Grand Dragon Calvin Craig, Governor Ross Barnett of Mississippi, and future Georgia governor Lester Maddox, lately hailed for driving black patrons from his restaurant with an ax handle and pistol. When two black members of the audience dared to jeer the racist speakers, they were mobbed and beaten with metal chairs while the crowd roared, "Kill 'em!" and "We want Wallace!"

Rowe had his own close call after the rally, at a meeting of Klan potentates where Robert Shelton informed him that another Eastview knight, Bill Holt, had branded Rowe an FBI informer. Grand Titan Robert Thomas concurred, but Shelton spoke in Rowe's defense, refusing to expel him from the UKA. Within eight months, the wizard would regret that choice.

The year's November vote for president disappointed racists nationwide. With Wallace out of the running by August, Shelton's UKA endorsed ultra-conservative Republican nominee Barry Goldwater, despite the fact that he was Jewish and his running mate was Catholic. Both disavowed the Klan's support, but Shelton forged ahead. On November 3, Johnson smothered Goldwater with a landslide of 42.8 million votes to 27.1 million. The NSRP's team of Kasper and Stoner polled a miserable 6,957 votes, down 97 percent from the party's showing in 1960.

Old Flames

Two months before the general election, on September 5 and 6, the UKA held a klonvocation in Birmingham, masked as a convention of the Alabama Rescue Service. Delegates re-elected wizard Robert Shelton as a matter of routine, then adopted a revised constitution for the order "in the Aulic of his Majesty, the Imperial Wizard." The sixty-nine-page document, ironically addressed to "the lovers of law, order, peace, and justice of all nations, people, tribes, and tongues of the whole earth," repeated the shopworn claim that the Klan's invisible empire "embrace[d] the whole world," while reiterating that membership was restricted to "White male Gentile person[s]" who were native-born Americans age twenty-one or older. Having thus reduced "the whole world" to some 2 percent of its total population, the UKA constitution rambled on through various procedures for enlistment, collection of fees, and discipline of rowdy members.

Such weighty matters hardly bothered the Klansmen of Eastview 13 that September. Gary Rowe was more concerned about Agent Blake's retirement and the imposition of a new handler, Agent Neil Shanahan, whom Blake deemed "very sharp...a type of person who would relate to Tommy right away." Shanahan later described himself in a sworn deposition as "a man of simple pleasures...[who] likes girls, smokes a pipe, drinks beer...a man's man." Blake described Rowe to his new bureau contact as "the best informant we had in the Ku Klux Klan."

On September 17, Klansman Ronnie Tidwell told Eastview's knights that "thrill-seeking beatniks" had been seen indulging in "race mixing" at the Flame Club, a black-owned bar in Fairfield. Nine days later, Rowe went to check it out with fellow Klansmen Curtis Doles, Cecil Hanson, and Eugene Thomas. Over beers, they were infuriated by "open displays of affection" between blacks and whites, including mixed-race parties "sitting together, dancing, kissing." As they left the club, Rowe later claimed, a Bessemer police car arrived with a Lieutenant Barnes at the wheel. Barnes listened to Thomas and Rowe, then asked, "What do you need?" Thomas replied, "Dynamite, hand grenades, and a submachine gun." Rowe claimed that Barnes left the club, then returned thirty minutes later to give the Klansmen a Tommy gun, eight sticks of dynamite, and six hand grenades from some unknown source.

Rowe and company drove their new arsenal back to Eastview and put out emergency calls to their brethren. Thirty-five Klansmen gathered in short order and a plan was hatched: two sticks of dynamite would be touched off at the Flame Club's backdoor, coordinated with grenades to drive the customers outside, where snipers would cut them down with the Tommy gun and other weapons. Returning to their target, they saw several Fairfield patrol cars nearby and retreated, vowing to return the next night. According to Rowe, Grand Titan Robert Thomas then postponed the raid until Saturday night, October 3.

Titan Thomas called Rowe back on September 29, reporting that Wizard Shelton deemed a wholesale massacre "politically inappropriate." Thomas asked Rowe to contact Jefferson County Deputy Sheriff Raymond Belcher and see if quasi-legal means could be used to close the Flame Club. On October 13, Deputy Belcher gave Rowe a supply of illegal pills and bootleg "wildcat" whiskey, which Rowe planted in the bar's restroom before tipping off agents of the state's Alcoholic Beverage Control Board. Officers raided the bar and shut it down on October 14. Eight days later, at Eastview's next meeting, Titan Thomas read a letter of commendation from Robert Shelton, praising the knights who "had discovered a dangerous situation of race mixing...at the Flame Club" and helped police resolve it "at personal disregard for their own safety and well-being."

Hectic Days

In early 1965, Birmingham Klansmen divided their time between side trips to Selma and action in their own backyard. Dallas County Sheriff Jim Clark, beginning his tenth year in office, had a reputation for brutality toward blacks, supported by the racist vigilantes of his "special posse." The local Hotel Albert accepted Dr. King and eleven companions as its first-ever black guests on January 18, but NSRP member James Robinson punched King as the minister tried to register. Police Chief Wilson Baker jailed Robinson, along with another NSRP member and two ranking officers of the American Nazi Party who invaded a rally at one of Selma's black churches. Sheriff Clark balanced the books on January 19 by arresting sixty-seven blacks who tried to register as voters. Beatings and more arrests followed, but Clark got the worst of it on January 25, when Annie Cooper, a 226-pound motel clerk, punched him in the eye. Three days later, Robert Thomas placed his Eastview knights on red alert, ordering Gary Rowe to draw up lists of local Klansmen and their weapons.

Dr. King's new campaign claimed its first life on February 18, when state troopers shot and fatally wounded unarmed protester Jimmy Lee Jackson at a demonstration in Marion, the seat of neighboring Perry County. Two days later, Governor Wallace belatedly announced his assignment of troopers to Dallas and Perry Counties, to prevent "any demonstration evidently conducted for the purpose of creating a breach of the peace." Wallace failed to mention that his troopers had been beating Jimmy Jackson's mother when he (Jackson) tried to intervene and thereby met his death.

On March 7, 525 black marchers gathered in Selma, prepared to walk forty miles to the state capital, there presenting a desegregation petition to Governor Wallace. Two hundred lawmen, state troopers, and Sheriff Clark's mounted posse, met them on the Edmund Pettus bridge with clubs, tear gas and bullwhips, sending sixty-eight protesters to the hospital. President Johnson condemned the brutality, while Wallace claimed the assault was required to preserve public safety.

State troopers attack nonviolent protesters on Selma's Edmund Pettus Bridge.
Credit: Library of Congress

Meanwhile, Klansmen in Jefferson County were distracted by trouble at Bessemer's W.S. Dickey Clay Manufacturing Company. Most of the plant's employees were black, supervised by sixteen white inspectors. In January 1965, those sixteen—led by Bessemer's exalted cyclops—petitioned the National Labor Relations Board for representation by the United Brick and Clay Workers Union. Their goal: creation of an all-white union local. Dickey's black workers called a strike in protest, and began picketing the plant on February 8. Ten days later, a bomb exploded at the plant, and a striker's car was blasted with shotguns. By March 12, when Dickey obtained an injunction against unlawful acts, more bombings had occurred, the plant's gas mains were sabotaged, and several trucks' fuel tanks were spiked with sugar. Violence continued after the injunction, including nine more bombings by August 9, plus gunfire damage to multiple employees' vehicles.

Congressional investigators subsequently blamed that violence on UKA members who were not employed at the Dickey plant, noting in particular the presence of Eastview klavern member Collie Leroy Wilkins, soon to be notorious in another context. Police made no arrests. The acts of terrorism at the Dickey plant remain officially unsolved.

On March 9, Dr. King led 1,500 marchers from Brown Chapel in Selma to the Edmund Pettus Bridge and across it, before troopers stopped the procession. No violence occurred this time, perhaps because white clergy from the North had joined the column. That night, three march participants—Rev. James Reeb from Boston, with Rev. Orloff Miller and Rev. John Wells, both from Washington, D.C.—were attacked and beaten by four white men armed with clubs, outside Selma's Silver Moon Café. Reeb suffered a fractured skull and died at a Birmingham hospital on March 11, without regaining consciousness.

Meanwhile, on March 10, Selma police jailed four suspects: Elmer Cook, Namon O'Neal Hoggle, brother William Stanley Hoggle, and R.B. Kelly. On April 13, despite presiding judge James Hare's preliminary rant against "nigras" and "self-appointed saints" meddling in Selma's troubles, a grand jury indicted Cook and the Hoggles for murder; Kelly denied participating in the beatings and was not charged, though FBI records report that a club was found in his car. Two weeks after their arrest, Eugene Thomas introduced Cook and the Hoggles to Gary Rowe as fellow members of the UKA. At their trial, on December 10, Sheriff Clark entered the jury room during deliberations, and the all-white, all-male panel soon emerged to acquit all three defendants.

In the interim, Birmingham's bombers were back in action, but without success. On Sunday, March 21, six unexploded bombs were found, each containing fifty sticks of dynamite and timers fashioned from alarm clocks. One, discovered at Our Lady, Queen of the Universe Catholic Church on Center Street, was discovered with services in progress and disarmed by an army team from Fort McClellan minutes before its scheduled detonation. While the soldiers were at work, a policeman found a second bomb at the home of Arthur Shores, then another surfaced in an alley behind the Gaston Funeral Home. At four o'clock several youths found the fifth bomb in an incinerator at all-black Western High School, in Ensley. The sixth, planted nearby at Rev. A.D.

King's former parsonage, proved to be a dud. FBI agents opened a new investigation, code-named GREENBOMBS, but it went nowhere. Police made no arrests, and Agent Shanahan received no leads from his crack informant. By that time, Gary Rowe was neck-deep in another crime— and this time it was murder.

"Bloody Lowndes"

Detroit homemaker Viola Gregg Liuzzo had been horrified by televised images of police brutality against Alabama protesters on March 7, 1965. Nine days later, she joined in a demonstration at Wayne State University, then called her husband to say that she was going to Selma. The movement there, she said, was "everybody's fight."

On March 17, after six days of public hearings, Judge Frank Johnson upheld the right of demonstrators to stage a peaceful march from Selma to Montgomery. He further enjoined Governor Wallace, along with other state and county authorities, from "harassing or threatening" the marchers. Johnson also ordered Wallace to provide police protection for the march. When Wallace demurred, pleading lack of men and funds, President Johnson federalized the National Guard, sending 1,863 guardsmen, 1,000 military police, 100 FBI agents and 100 U.S. marshals to keep order in Alabama.

Thirty-two hundred marchers set out from Selma on March 21, reaching the governor's mansion on March 25. Wallace refused to accept their petition, peering at the mass of demonstrators from his office window through binoculars, and the demonstrators began to disperse. Viola Liuzzo volunteered to drive small groups back to Selma in her personal car. Tragedy struck on her second round-trip, on Highway 80 in Lowndes County—called "Bloody Lowndes" for its history of violence. There, at 8 p.m., gunshots from another car killed Liuzzo instantly, leaving her passenger, nineteen-year-old Leroy Moton, uninjured. Moton told police that two cars had pursued Liuzzo's on the highway, one returning after she was shot, at which time he played dead to save himself.

On March 26, President Johnson appeared on television with J. Edgar Hoover, announcing the arrest of four Klansmen on federal charges of conspiring to violate Liuzzo's civil rights. LBJ identified the suspects as William Orville Eaton, Eugene Thomas, Collie Leroy Wilkins—and Gary Thomas Rowe. A federal grand jury formally indicted Eaton, Thomas, and Wilkins on April 6, while filing no charge against Rowe. Lowndes County's grand jury indicted the trio for first-degree murder on April

22. By then, UKA leaders knew the worst: Gary Rowe was a federal spy, scheduled to testify against his fellow knights at trial.

Efforts to smear Liuzzo and blame her for her own slaying began almost immediately. On March 26, learning that Liuzzo's husband was a Teamsters Union official, Sheriff Clark phoned a Michigan acquaintance, Warren Police Commissioner Marvin Lane, to request information on Liuzzo's family. (Clark claimed he had been threatened by an anonymous Teamster, but he produced no evidence of any such threat.) Lane contacted Detroit police, who found a misdemeanor conviction resulting from Viola's challenge to the state's compulsory school statute and compiled a litany of rumors from unfriendly neighbors, sending the material on to Clark. From Selma, the report found its way to Al Lingo, and then to Imperial Wizard Shelton, who broadcast false claims that Liuzzo had suffered from syphilis. (Earlier, Shelton had claimed—again, falsely—that Rev. James Reeb was dying from cancer, as if that somehow excused his murder.)

Viola Liuzzo, murdered by Klansmen, then slandered by the FBI. *Credit: Library of Congress*

The FBI was no better. On orders from headquarters, Birmingham agent Spencer Robb released a bureau memo claiming (again, falsely) that Liuzzo "had puncture marks in her arms indicating recent use of a hypodermic needle." J. Edgar Hoover, in his personal briefing to President Johnson, passed along the fabricated observation that Liuzzo had been "sitting very, very close to the Negro in the car. It had the appearance of a necking party."

For all its negligence in handling Gary Rowe, the bureau still took fierce offense at any charge of impropriety—as on March 27, when Sheriff Clark accused G-men of withholding information on surveillance of Liuzzo's killers. State troopers had stopped Eugene Thomas's car two hours before the shooting, Clark revealed. Liuzzo "might not have been murdered," he said, if the bureau had told him "they had that car under surveillance." Hoover fired back, calling Clark's statement "a malicious lie...typical of his weakness in handling his responsibilities."

Before the first Liuzzo indictments were handed down, on April 1, another bomb rocked one of Birmingham's black neighborhoods, wounding one resident with shattered window glass. One the same day, unexploded bombs were found at the homes of Mayor Boutwell and City Councilwoman Nina Miglionico, perceived by racists as a "moderate."

Trial and Error

Collie Wilkins was first to face trial for Liuzzo's murder in Hayneville, defended by UKA Imperial Klonsel Matthew Hobson Murphy, Jr. Robert Shelton attended the trial, and sometimes sat at the defense table, normally reserved for legal counsel. The trial convened on May 4 and offered Gary Rowe's first public testimony as a prosecution witness. He described Eugene Thomas driving the murder car, overtaking Liuzzo's vehicle and shouting, "All right, men, shoot the hell out of it!"

Wilkins and William Eaton both shot at the car, Rowe said, while he stuck his gun out the window and shook it, pretending to fire. Afterward, Rowe saw the target car still following, before it swerved off-road, and suggested the bullets had missed. "Baby brother," Wilkins replied, "I don't miss. That bitch and that bastard are dead and in Hell."

On cross-examination, Murphy damned Rowe for violating his Klan oath and taking FBI money. County prosecutors acknowledged their support for segregation, but still asked the all-white jury—including several admitted Citizens' Council members—to find Wilkins guilty of murder. Murphy's hysterical summation ranged from attacks on the United Nations and NAACP to "nigger" prosecution witness Leroy Moton.

Robert Shelton (left) with
"klonsel" Matt Murphy at the
first Liuzzo murder trial.
Credit: National Archives

Then the nigger ran up the road and a
truck came by and he stopped it. There
was a rabbi in that truck. A rabbi! Of
course, he stopped and put the nigger
in the back. And there they were—rabbi
with a nigger ... white woman, nigger
man, nigger woman—all in there,
feet to feet....Integration breaks every
moral law God ever wrote....That's
God's law. I don't care what Lyndon Johnson or anybody else says.

Jurors deliberated for ten hours, then reported a hopeless deadlock
with ten voting guilty on a reduced charge of manslaughter, while two
stood firm for acquittal. Judge Thomas Thagard declared a mistrial and
scheduled Wilkins for retrial at a later date. Neither side mentioned the
second pursuit car described by Leroy Moton and widely reported by
the media.

Matt Murphy would not live to see the second trial. At 3:45 a.m. on
August 20, 1965, while driving from Birmingham to UKA headquarters
in Tusccaloosa, he struck an asphalt tanker truck and died instantly in
his shattered car. Subsequent investigation proved Murphy was drinking
heavily at Birmingham's Patio Bar before the accident. His place would
be taken at future Liuzzo trials by attorney Arthur Hanes, Sr.—Murphy's
former college roommate, who also served as one of his pall bearers.

A "Special" Deputy

News of Murphy's death was overshadowed by reports of another
Klan killing in Lowndes County on August 20. The latest victim,
Massachusetts seminary student Jonathan Myrick Daniels, had come to
Alabama on the same plane that carried James Reeb, back in March.
Daniels had spent some time in Dallas County, but had not participated
in the Selma-to-Montgomery march. Instead, he wound up as the first

white civil rights worker in Bloody Lowndes, joined subsequently by Catholic priest Richard Morrisroe. Both were arrested on August 14, during a demonstration at Fort Deposit, and were jailed in Hayneville until winning release at 3 p.m. on August 20.

From jail, Daniels and Morrisroe proceeded to a nearby store, accompanied by two black girls. At the store, they were confronted by a white man with a shotgun, who refused them entry, then shot both clergymen at close range. Daniels died on the spot, while Morrisroe would survive despite critical wounds.

The shooter, Tom Lemuel Coleman, was a member of Hayneville's most prominent family. His father had been sheriff of the county and its former school superintendent, the latter post held in 1965 by Tom's sister. Coleman himself carried credentials as a "special deputy" to current Sheriff Frank Ryals. An engineer for the state highway department, Coleman was also a close friend of Sheriff Jim Clark and Al Lingo, who employed Coleman's son as a state trooper. Six years before the Hayneville shooting, on August 21, 1959, Coleman had shot and killed a black prisoner at Greenville's prison camp, when guards professed themselves unable to handle the inmate.

Aside from his dubious police work, Coleman was a hard-drinking member of the Citizens' Council, outspoken in his opposition to black civil rights. He denied Klan membership, but substantial evidence suggests direct involvement with the KKK. In early 1965, he had confronted Alabama Attorney General Richmond Flowers at Hayneville's courthouse, demanding that Flowers "get off the Ku Klux Klan and get on these outfits down here trying to get these niggers registered [to vote]. If you don't get off this Klan investigation, we'll get you off." Author Taylor Branch also reports that Coleman was among a party of "familiar Klansmen" who, armed with rifles and shotguns, raided all-black Mt. Carmel Baptist Church in Lowndes County on February 28, 1965, threatening its minister and members for their civil rights work.

After shooting Daniels and Morrisroe, Coleman walked to the nearby courthouse, where he took the first call reporting the incident. (Sheriff Ryals was "out of town.") Moments later, Coleman phoned Al Lingo in Montgomery, saying, "I just shot two preachers. You'd better get down here." Lingo hastened to his friend's aid, accompanied by a bail bondsman whom Richmond Flowers described as a known Klan member. From that day forward, Lingo's office stonewalled Flowers and the FBI in their pursuit of information on the case.

Authorities charged Coleman with first-degree murder of Daniels, and assault with intent to commit murder on Morrisroe. At a farcical trial in September, where Coleman's own name appeared on a list of prospective jurors, Judge Thagard excluded Richmond Flowers from the case, leaving the trial to a local prosecutor who reduced the charge from murder to manslaughter. With Viola Liuzzo's killers in the spectators' gallery, that same prosecutor seemed to accept defense claims that victims Daniels and Morrisroe had been armed with a knife and pistol, respectively, when Coleman shot them "in self-defense." Both weapons had vanished, meanwhile, presumably taken by unknown black bystanders.

It came as no surprise to anyone when Coleman's all-white jury acquitted him of manslaughter on September 30. The case involving victim Morrisroe—still recuperating from his wounds in another state—was dismissed without trial in May 1966. On hearing that verdict, Richmond Flowers declared, "Even illiterate Negroes in Lowndes County are speed readers of handwriting on the wall. They know that the Klan is riding in Alabama today."

Liuzzo Redux

Flowers himself served as prosecutor at the second trial of Collie Wilkins, convened on October 18, 1965. He called his case "the strongest I've ever had," including Gary Rowe's eyewitness testimony, but it went awry from the start. The jury seated by Judge Thagard included one former Klansman and eight past or present members of the Citizens' Council; eleven of the twelve admitted believing that blacks were inferior to whites, and several openly praised the Klan. When Flowers appealed for their dismissal on grounds of racial bias, Alabama's Supreme Court refused.

The strong case went downhill from there. While Art Hanes abstained from Murphy's bizarre theatrics, he still implied "touching" between Liuzzo and Leroy Moton, confused Moton in his description of the killers' vehicle, and elicited an admission from the state's forensic expert that he could not say whether Liuzzo was shot from a moving car or "from the ground."

Before Rowe took the stand a second time, FBI agents stunned Flowers by demanding a grant of immunity from prosecution for their informant. Flowers agreed, while advising the G-men that he could not bind future attorneys general with his promise. In court, Rowe repeated his description of the shooting, then admitted under cross-examination that he had made no attempt to prevent the Liuzzo shooting. While reporters generally praised Rowe's performance on the witness stand, Flowers feared that his testimony had little impact on the racist jury.

Liuzzo murder defendants William Eaton, Eugene Thomas, and Collie Wilkins (left to right) sign autographs at a Klan rally.
Credit: National Archives

Hanes presented a brief defense case. Two state troopers testified that Moton had described the killers' car as an "old Ford," rather than a Chevrolet, and two employees of a Bessemer saloon placed Wilkins and company at the bar between 8:45 and 9 p.m. on March 25—an impossible drive if they shot Liuzzo at 8, 140 miles away.

On October 22, both sides presented their summations to the jury. While Flowers stressed Rowe's testimony, Hanes described the case as a "parable of the two goats—the Judas goat and the scapegoat." Rowe was the Judas, likened to "one of the most loathsome characters in all of history," while Wilkins was the innocent patsy. Most likely, Hanes said, Liuzzo was killed by civil rights workers to give the movement a martyr. "Maybe the murderer is from the Watts area of Los Angeles," Hanes said, alluding to California's recent ghetto riot, or else hiding in Georgia, "trying to raise money for their nefarious schemes." The jurors agreed, deliberating for less than two hours before they acquitted Wilkins.

In the wake of that verdict, Klansmen plastered their cars with newly-printed bumper stickers reading "OPEN SEASON," but their celebration was short-lived. On November 5, 1965, a federal grand jury indicted Eaton, Thomas and Wilkins on charges of conspiring to violate Liuzzo's civil rights. When the new trial convened on April 6, 1966, Judge Frank

Johnson presided in Montgomery, refusing to accept a jury infested with Klansmen and Citizens' Council members. The panel convicted all three defendants, whereupon they received the maximum federal term of ten years imprisonment.

State murder trials of Liuzzo's killers continued to disappoint observers over the next eleven months. William Eaton died from an apparent heart attack on March 9, 1966, with his federal verdict on appeal and his state case still pending. Eugene Thomas faced trial before a jury of eight blacks and four whites on September 29, 1966, but Richmond Flowers failed to call Gary Rowe or Leroy Moton as witnesses, resulting in acquittal by day's end.

Governor Wallace, oblivious to the judicial travesties in Lowndes County, declared, "We've got good law enforcement in Alabama." He felt obliged to add, "Of course, if I did what I'd like to do I'd pick up something and smash one of these federal judges in the head and then burn the courthouse down. But I'm too genteel."

A New Day

"Genteel" or not, Wallace was running out of time as governor, barred from a second consecutive term by state law. His scheme to circumvent that barrier had worked before—in Texas, four decades earlier—for disgraced governor James Ferguson. Wallace's wife, Lurleen, would run for office in his place. Her term, if she succeeded, would grant Wallace four more years in which to change the rules and make himself invincible.

The Klan signed on to help as it had done in 1962. Bob Chambliss was among the more active political knights, campaigning both for Lurleen Wallace and for close friend and fellow UACG member Robert Gafford, seeking a seat in the state legislature. Nine other candidates challenged Mrs. Wallace in the May 3 Democratic primary, but she swept the field with 480,841 votes, while her nearest rival—Richmond Flowers—polled 172,386 and former Klan crony John Patterson placed sixth with 31,011. On November 8, in the general election, Lurleen Wallace triumphed with 537,505 ballots to Republican James Martin's 262,943 and independent Carl Robinson's 47,653.

Lurleen Wallace campaigns for governor, on her husband's behalf.
Credit: Library of Congress

The Wallace margin of victory surprised some observers, since the Voting Rights Act— inspired by Alabama violence and signed by President Johnson on August 6, 1965—had permitted registration of 122,000 new black voters statewide, but victory was only won by increments. Bob Gafford—who provided Hubert Page's alibi for the Sixteenth Street bombing, and who later attended the Cahaba Bridge meeting—won the first of four terms in Alabama's House of Representatives, serving through 1982, when he lost a bid for the state senate. Notable losers in 1966 were Jim Clark, seeking re-election as sheriff in Dallas County, and Al Lingo, defeated in a bid to become sheriff of Jefferson County.

The deposed symbols of "law and order" enjoyed mixed fortunes after leaving office. Lingo died in Birmingham, in August 1969, at age fifty-nine. Clark worked odd jobs, toured as a speaker for the John Birch Society, then pled guilty to smuggling marijuana in 1978, received a two-year prison term, and served nine months. Upon release, he sold mobile homes until his death in 2007.

Business As Usual

Despite political shifts in the Cotton State, Klan-type violence continued unabated. On January 3, 1966, a white gas station attendant in Macon County shot and killed black civil rights activist Samuel Younge, Jr., pleading self-defense. Witnesses reported that Younge had asked to use the station's restroom and was refused, then gunned down. The usual all-white jury acquitted his killer on December 8, 1966.

In Birmingham, meanwhile, a white motorist fired eight shots into a crowd of 150 black demonstrators on February 21, 1966. The gunman surrendered and confessed, facing five counts of assault with intent to kill, but the case was dismissed when he claimed self-defense, alleging that the wounded victims tried to drag him from his car before he opened fire.

Two days later, on February 23, Jefferson County Sheriff Mel Bailey announced that an unnamed local resident had found a "bomb factory" in the woods outside Birmingham, back on February 19. The cache included several cases of dynamite and one timing device identical to those retrieved from bombs planted around the city in April 1965.

No arrests resulted from the seizure of explosives, and the would-be bombers remained at large. In fact, they struck again on February 24, detonating two blasts that damaged a formerly all-white school in Elba, Alabama. The school had admitted its first two black students in September 1965, but Klansmen had bided their time. By luck or by design, the February bombing failed to claim any lives, though 200 potential victims had left the campus a short time earlier, after attending a banquet in the school's cafeteria.

Chapter 10
Justice Deferred

While Lurleen Wallace settled into the governor's office, Robert Shelton and three of his grand dragons received one-year federal prison terms for contempt of Congress, after withholding Klan records from the House Committee on Un-American Activities. Lurleen's term was cut short when cancer claimed her life in May 1968, leaving Lieutenant Governor Albert Brewer in charge.

Another presidential race helped distract George Wallace from his grief. Running this time on behalf of the new American Independent Party—a far-right collection of Klansmen, Citizens' Council members, John Birchers, and neo-Nazis—Wallace chose retired Air Force General Curtis LeMay as his running mate after rebuffs from ex-Kentucky governor Happy Chandler and Kentucky Fried Chicken founder "Colonel" Harland Sanders. Vowing "law and order," plus an end to the Vietnam war if it could not be won within ninety days, Wallace polled nearly ten million votes and carried five southern states, but Richard Nixon's "southern strategy" and secret deals defeated him.

In 1970, supported by a new fiancée, Wallace launched his third gubernatorial campaign. Robert Shelton's UKA supported him, while Governor Brewer courted black votes and five other candidates muddied the waters, Ace Carter among them. Brewer led Wallace by a narrow margin in May's primary election—428,146 votes to 416,443, while Carter polled 15,441. In the runoff, Wallace collected those ballots and enough others to beat Brewer by a margin of 559,832 to 525,951. In November's general election, after a blatantly racist campaign, Wallace triumphed with 74.5 percent of all ballots cast.

The governor's mind, however, was still fixed on Washington. He launched another presidential campaign in January 1972, running again for the AIP, but a bungled assassination attempt left him crippled in May. Lieutenant Governor Jere Beasley—a friend of the Klan in his own right, who addressed the UKA's 1970 klonvocation—served as acting governor until July, when Wallace emerged from a Maryland hospital. The AIP's replacement presidential candidate, California Bircher-congressman

John Schmitz, polled 1.1 million votes in November without carrying a single state.

The Klan, meanwhile, had shrunken in size and influence, despite friendship with Beasley and Alabama Senator James Allen, who autographed a photo: "With sincerest best wishes to my good friend Robert M. Shelton." Despite eternal confidence, the terrorists of Birmingham were running out of time.

Headline announcing George Wallace's survival of his shooting in May 1972.
Credit: National Archives

Never Too Late

William Joseph Baxley II was a 22-year-old law student at the University of Alabama when Klansmen bombed the Sixteenth Street Baptist Church. After two terms as district attorney in Dothan, he won election as Alabama's attorney general in 1970, and soon reopened the BAPBOMB case. Obstructed by the FBI, which doggedly refused to share its files, Baxley pursued a list of suspects that included Gary Rowe, subjecting those who would submit to polygraph exams. Three probable participants—John Hall, Ross Keith, and Troy Ingram—died before Baxley could quiz them, but others remained.

A visit to Washington, with parents of the murdered girls in tow, cracked the FBI roadblock in 1976, providing evidence enough to charge Bob Chambliss with the fatal bombing, while Jesse Stoner was indicted for the 1958 blast at Bethel Baptist Church. Writing from Georgia, Stoner branded Baxley an "honorary nigger." Baxley replied, on official stationery:

> My response to your letter of February 19, 1976, is—kiss my ass.

Indicted for the murder of Denise McNair on September 26, 1977, Chambliss pled not guilty on October 28, and proceeded to trial on November 14. State witnesses included his niece, Elizabeth Hood Cobbs, now a Methodist minister. Defense attorney Arthur Hanes challenged each witness in turn, but they proved unshakable. Jurors convicted Dynamite Bob on November 18—his victim's birthday—and he received a life prison term. Nine days later, Baxley announced his intent to charge more suspects in the bombing.

It was not to be, although he did have Jesse Stoner. Indicted on September 27, 1977, for the Shuttlesworth bombing, Stoner appealed Governor George Busbee's extradition order and found a Georgia judge willing to overturn it in November 1978. By then, Stoner had launched a gubernatorial race designed to unseat Busbee and immunize himself against extradition. Busbee prevailed, with 80.7 percent of the popular vote, and Georgia's Supreme Court upheld Stoner's extradition in July 1979. After six months in hiding, Stoner surrendered in Birmingham on January 11, 1980.

Before his trial convened in May, Stoner took another fling at politics, announcing plans to challenge Georgia Senator Herman Talmadge. Crushed in the Democratic primary, Stoner proceeded to trial on May 12, facing Sgt. Tom Cook and other witnesses who described his contract bombing of Bethel Baptist Church two decades earlier. Jurors convicted Stoner on May 14, resulting in a ten-year sentence. His plea for a new trial was denied on September 12, and Georgia's bar association suspended him from practicing law on November 9. Following rejection of his last appeal in October 1984, Stoner spent another four months on the lam, then surrendered to share a prison cell with Bob Chambliss. Chambliss died on October 29, 1985, and Stoner was paroled the following year, to lead a new extremist movement—the Crusade Against Corruption—that campaigned against homosexuality under the slogan "Thank God for AIDS!"

Out of prison and unrepentant, Jess Stoner leads the Klan
in a "Crusade Against Corruption."
Credit: National Archives

False Hope

Hopes for prosecution of more Birmingham bombers arose in October 1988, when former Klansman Gary Tucker contacted FBI agents to "clear his conscience" concerning the Sixteenth Street blast. Dying of cancer at age fifty-four, Tucker confessed to personally planting the charge and setting its timer on the night of September 14, 1963. According to vague media reports, he also named others involved in the plot.

Justice Department spokesman Mark Weaver, speaking to the *New York Times* on October 18, declared:

> We are checking his information against our files and we want to meet with him again this week.

The story hit a snag when one of Tucker's relatives alleged he had been diagnosed as schizophrenic and hospitalized several times for "emotional problems." Local authorities countered by saying that Tucker "seems to know a lot of stuff that would have only been known by somebody who was involved" in the bombing. On October 21, state authorities said that Tucker had identified another suspect, left unnamed in media reports, but survivors of the bombing victims waited in vain for indictments.

Exit Gary Rowe

Gary Rowe's behavior as an FBI informer haunted bureau headquarters long after he vanished into the federal witness protection system. He surfaced in December 1975, barely disguised by a Klan-type mask, to testify before a U.S. Senate committee investigating criminal activities of the FBI and CIA. In that televised appearance, Rowe claimed that his handlers had ordered him to "try to sleep with as many [Klan] wives as I could"—more than a dozen, by his count—to disrupt their families and obtain meaty gossip through "pillow talk."

In Birmingham, Detective Red Self told the *Post-Herald:*

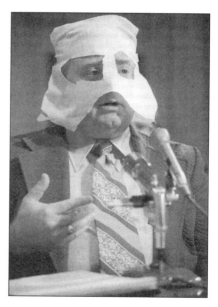

Gary Rowe testifies before the U.S. Senate in disguise.
Credit: National Archives

> Tommy Rowe will do almost anything to get some attention. There is not one word of truth in what he is saying.

Tom Cook, now a lieutenant, agreed that Rowe was "a compulsive liar... an oddball. Wants notoriety all the time...and would do anything to get it." Black city councilman Richard Arrington sought a full investigation of local police, but his motion was defeated after furious debate.

In summer 1978, the CBS news program *20/20* aired a segment on Viola Liuzzo's murder, wherein ex-Klansmen Collie Wilkins and Eugene Thomas named Rowe as the triggerman. Both passed polygraph tests, while Rowe's test results indicated deception. July brought news that Alabama authorities considered Rowe a bombing suspect, but they ultimately filed no charges.

In July 1979, the Liuzzo family filed a $2 million lawsuit charging the FBI with complicity in Viola's murder. Trial convened on March 21, 1983, with testimony from convicted conspirators Wilkins and Thomas (who had "found God" in prison), ex-Attorney General Ramsey Clark, Birmingham policemen Lavaughn Coleman and Henry Snow, and Flossie Creel, widow of Alabama's 1960s UKA grand dragon (claiming that her late husband named Rowe as Liuzzo's slayer). The defense alleged a plot by Klansmen and police to punish Rowe for his role as a turncoat. Judge Charles Joiner dismissed the case on May 27, 1983, officially clearing Rowe as a murder suspect.

Meanwhile, freedom riders Walter Bergman and James Peck separately sued the FBI in January 1983, seeking damages of $1 million and $500,000 respectively for their 1963 injuries, on grounds that the bureau knew of Klan plans to attack the integrated buses and did nothing to prevent it. Both won their cases, but at discounted rates, with Peck awarded $25,000 and Bergman receiving $35,000.

By then, the bureau's brawler was running out of time. After years of working as a private detective—and, incredibly, as a deputy U.S. marshal in California—Rowe died bankrupt in Savannah, Georgia, on May 25, 1998. According to his *New York Times* obituary, he was survived by five children, their identities concealed "for obvious reasons."

Fatal Echoes

At Rowe's death, no more charges had been filed in Birmingham's long series of racist bombings. The statute of limitations had expired in most cases, except for the Sixteenth Street blast that resulted in multiple murder. J. Edgar Hoover formally closed the FBI's file on that crime in 1971, the year before his death, and his successors had done their best to obstruct Bill Baxley's prosecution of Bob Chambliss five years later.

Twelve years after that, Robert Langford was named agent-in-charge of the bureau's Birmingham field office. After meeting with black leaders, he sent clerks to search the office's dusty files, where they found ninety volumes of investigative records from the Sixties, each containing hundreds of documents. The files fingered Chambliss, Thomas Blanton Jr., Herman Cash, and Bobby Frank Cherry as prime suspects in the fatal blast, but Cash died in February 1994, before the old files were retrieved.

That left two bombers at large, but what could be done with them three decades after their crime? Since 1963, 140 witnesses of other persons central to the bombing case had either died or been declared incompetent. More time elapsed, and Agent Langford retired in 1996, succeeded by Joseph Louis. The bureau formally announced its reopening of the BAPBOMB case on July 11, 1997, declaring that "the main suspects [from 1963] were still the suspects." But was there evidence sufficient to indict them?

Agent Bob Herren traced Bobby Lee Cherry to Texas in 1997, recording his denial of involvement in the fatal bombing. Cherry *did* admit to beating Fred Shuttlesworth with brass knuckles in 1957, but insisted that the Klan would never bomb churches because it was a Christian organization. To prove his point, Cherry claimed that he "sang in the Klan choir at churches and funerals." His main reason for joining the KKK, Cherry said, was that he "wanted to chase women when he went to Klan rallies."

Soon after speaking to Herren, Cherry granted an interview to crusading Mississippi journalist Jerry Mitchell. In that conversation, Cherry offered an alibi for September 14, 1963: He'd spent the night at home with his wife, watching televised wrestling matches. Mitchell checked the TV schedule for the night in question and found that no wrestling had aired.

In Alabama, Cherry's granddaughter—Teresa Stacy—read the interview, later telling reporters, "I knew he was lying." She recalled conversations from her childhood, wherein Cherry said "he helped blow up a bunch of niggers back in Birmingham. He seemed rather jovial." Nor was she alone, noting that other relatives had "heard it for years." Finally outraged, Stacy told the *New York Times*:

> I called the news people. They put me on hold for a long time. I hung up the phone and called the FBI.

Cherry's ex-wife was also talking. During their marriage, she had quarreled with Bobby Lee about his snoring, staying up one night to tape the noise he made as proof. Aside from snores, the recorder also caught Cherry talking in his sleep about the Sixteenth Street bombing. That tape, she said, was lost in a house fire, but Cherry's ex was willing to testify against him.

Finally, the FBI unearthed its own ancient tapes from interviews in the Sixties, "virtually inaudible" at first, but partially improved by modern enhancement techniques. Those tapes, collected from bugs placed in the homes and cars of Klansmen, included several self-incriminating comments made by Tommy Blanton, Jr. If the tapes were deemed admissible, the prosecution had a case.

Round Two

On May 18, 2000, Birmingham's grand jury charged Bobby Cherry and Tom Blanton, Jr. with murder. Whereas Bob Chambliss had faced only one count, the latest defendants faced eight: one charge of intentional murder per victim, plus four counts of murder "with universal malice." Both defendants were jailed without bond, reporters noting that Cherry's eight-by-ten cell was larger than the trailer he had lately occupied in Texas. U.S. Attorney Doug Jones, on loan from Justice to assist state prosecutors, had skipped classes at law school to attend the Chambliss trial in 1977. Now, squared off against Dynamite Bob's old cronies, Jones refused to discuss claims that he had offered Cherry leniency in exchange for a guilty plea to lesser charges.

That hardly seemed to matter in April 2001, when Judge James Garrett pronounced Cherry "too demented to stand trial." That April 16th ruling, issued less than a week before Cherry's trial was supposed to begin, sidelined his case pending medical determination of his sanity. Meanwhile, the state would prosecute Tom Blanton, Jr. alone.

That trial convened on April 25, with Doug Jones sketching Birmingham's civil rights struggle for jurors. "There were people," he said, "and Thomas E. Blanton was one of them, who saw their segregated way of life dissolving and couldn't stand it." Defense attorney John Robbins warned, "You're not going to like Tom Blanton. You're not going to like some of the things he said. He was 25 years old. He was a loudmouth. He was annoying. He was a segregationist and he ran his mouth about that. He was a thorn in the FBI's side. He was annoying as hell. Just because you don't like him and the views he espoused doesn't make him responsible for this tragedy."

To prove that case, Jones played the FBI's tape of Blanton telling his wife that he missed their date on September 13, 1963, to meet fellow Klansmen under the Cahaba River bridge and "plan the bomb. You have to have a meeting to make a bomb." Another tape caught Blanton telling FBI informer Mitchell Burns that police would not catch him "when I bomb my next church." Referring to the Sixteenth Street blast, Burns asked, "How did you do that, Tommy?" Blanton's reply: "It wasn't easy, I tell you."

The defense called only two witnesses. One described a car decorated with Confederate flags, bearing no resemblance to Blanton's Chevrolet, seen near the church on the night of September 14. The other, former G-man William Fleming, viewed a photo of convicted bomber Jesse Stoner, granting that he bore some resemblance to Blanton, but Jones countered by noting that Stoner's photo was included in a batch shown to state witness James Lay—who chose Blanton's mug shot as the likeness of a man seen lurking near the church. In his summation, Robbins claimed that Blanton's boasts of bombing churches had been "taken out of context."

Jurors disagreed, deliberating a mere two hours on May 2, before they convicted Blanton on four murder counts. Each charge carried an automatic life sentence. Asked by Judge Garrett for any parting words, Blanton replied, "I guess the good Lord will settle on Judgment Day."

Thomas Blanton, Jr. leaves court following his murder conviction.
Credit: National Archives

End Game

Bobby Cherry's hope of avoiding prosecution ended on May 30, 2001, when a state psychologist found him mentally competent for trial. Even so, legal maneuvers delayed that trial until May 14, 2002, when a jury was seated to hear the case. Prosecution witnesses included the mothers of victims Denise McNair and Carol Robertson, plus Sarah Jean Rudolph (née Collins), describing the death of her sister. FBI informer Mitchell Burns produced more tapes, including one of a meeting where unidentified Klansman joked about being asked, "Where were you when the church blew up?" One responded, amidst laughter, "It wasn't us. We were trying to get ours ready for the weekend." The tape also included mention of the late Troy Ingram's name. Cherry remarked, "They think we made the bomb somewhere else."

So far, the state's links between Cherry and the fatal blast were tenuous. Stronger evidence came from his ex-wife, Willadean Brogdon, who recalled Cherry's boasting of participation in the crime throughout their marriage, during 1970-73. Brogdon also tied Cherry to Robert Chambliss and Tom Blanton, Jr., testifying that they "were all together the night the bomb was built." Granddaughter Teresa Stacy recalled similar statements, noting that Cherry "seemed rather jovial, braggish about it." A third witness—Texas house-painter Michael Goings, who worked with Cherry in 1982—also remembered the defendant saying, "You know, I bombed that church."

Defense attorney Mickey Johnson dismissed Brogdon as an embittered woman, ridiculing her claim that a tape of Cherry's confession was lost when their home burned, but jurors were convinced. On May 23, they convicted Cherry on four counts of murder, mandating four terms of life imprisonment. Before leaving the court in handcuffs, Cherry told Judge Garrett:

> This whole bunch have lied all through this thing. I've told the truth. I don't know why I'm going to jail for nothing. I didn't do anything.

Bobby Lee Cherry at trial.
Credit: National Archives

Both elderly bombers appealed their convictions. The Alabama Court of Criminal Appeals upheld Tom Blanton's verdict on September 11, 2003. The same court denied Bobby Cherry's appeal on October 2, 2004. Cherry died in prison seven weeks later, on November 18, 2004. At this writing, Blanton remains imprisoned at the St. Clair Correctional Facility in Springville, Alabama.

"Closure is Just a Word"

Following Blanton's conviction, reporters asked Carole Robertson's mother if the verdict had brought closure to her family. Alpha Robertson replied:

> Closure? I have often wondered why they associate that word with this affair. For those who are not involved, it is easy to say that. Closure is just a word.

And indeed, some observers suggest that the BAPBOMB case is still not closed. Foremost among them is Elizabeth Cobb, niece of Robert Chambliss whose testimony helped send him to prison. In her memoir of the case, *Long Time Coming* (1994), Cobb wrote

> There are police reports that indicate that two and perhaps three carloads of white men were in the area of the Sixteenth Street Baptist Church in the wee hours of Sunday, September 15, 1963: the car that Robert [Chambliss] was in, one with six members of the National States Rights Party, and another with at least two men who were said to be wearing police uniforms.

If true—and allowing for the deaths of two alleged and one confessed BAPBOMB participants—who were the other men? Are any still alive?

Reports of a "limping man" seen near the church might point to Jesse Stoner, but we cannot ask him now. Stoner died at a nursing home in LaFayette, Georgia, at age 83, on April 23, 2005.

We cannot ask Bull Connor. He suffered a stroke on February 26, 1973, and died twelve days later without regaining consciousness.

We cannot ask Al Lingo, dead since August 1969, or ex-Governor Wallace, lost to septic shock from a bacterial infection at Montgomery's Jackson Hospital on September 13, 1998.

The Cahaba Boys are lost to us: Ross Keith died in November 1965, Troy Ingram in May 1997, Charles Cagle in November 2004, and Herman Cash in January 2007. Of the UKA loyalists with possible BAPBOMB knowledge, Hubert Page died in May 1984, Ronnie Tidwell in September 1992, Floyd Simpson in February 1998, Don Luna in October 1999, and Levi Yarbrough in May 2006.

Art Hanes, Sr., the Klan's ablest defender, died in May 1997. Patrolman Floyd Garrett, nephew of Robert Chambliss, followed in February 1998.

Nor can we ask Robert Shelton, wizard of the United Klans, felled by a heart attack in Tuscaloosa at age 73, on March 17, 2003. Sixteen years before his death, Shelton saw the UKA bankrupted by wrongful-death litigation, filed in the case of Michael Donald, an African American lynched by two of Shelton's knights in 1981. That trial cost Shelton $7 million that he did not have, forcing surrender of his headquarters to Donald's mother. Both lynchers—Michael Hays and James "Tiger" Knowles—were convicted of murder. Knowles turned state's evidence and received a life sentence. Hays died by lethal injection on June 6, 1997, the first white person executed in Alabama since 1913 for slaying a black victim.

In Alabama and throughout the USA, the Ku Klux Klan endures.

Bibliography

Ames, Jessie. *The Changing Character of Lynching*. Atlanta: Commission of Interracial Cooperation, 1942.

Bartley, Numan. *The Rise of Massive Resistance*. Baton Rouge: Louisiana State University Press, 1997.

Bishop, Jim. *The Days of Martin Luther King, Jr.* New York: G.P. Putnam's Sons, 1971.

Branch, Taylor. *At Canaan's Edge*. New York: Simon & Schuster, 2006.

—. *Parting the Waters*. New York: Simon & Schuster, 1988.

—. *Pillar of Fire*. New York: Simon & Schuster, 1998.

Carter, Dan. *The Politics of Rage*. Baton Rouge: Louisiana State University Press, 2000.

Chalmers, David. *Backfire*. Lanham, MD: Rowman & Littlefield, 2003.

—. *Hooded Americanism* 3rd ed. Durham: Duke University Press, 1987.

Clark, E. Culpepper. *The Schoolhouse Door*. New York: Oxford University Press, 1993.

Cobbs, Elizabeth, and Petric Smith. *Long Time Coming*. Birmingham: Crane Hill, 1994.

Cook. James. *The Segregationists*. New York: Appleton-Century-Crofts, 1962.

Donner, Frank. *Protectors of Privilege*. Berkeley: University of California Press, 1990.

Eagles, Charles. *Outside Agitator*. Chapel Hill: University of North Carolina Press, 1993.

Encyclopedia of Alabama, http://encyclopediaofalabama.org/face/Home.jsp.

Feldman, Glenn. "The Ku Klux Klan in Alabama, 1915-1954." Ph.D. thesis, Auburn University, 1996.

—. *Politics, Society, and the Klan in Alabama, 1915-1949*. Tuscaloosa: University of Alabama Press, 1999.

—. "Soft Opposition: Elite Acquiescence and Klan-Sponsored Terrorism in Alabama, 1946-1950)." *The Historical Journal* (September 1997): 753-77.

Flowers, Richmond. "Southern Plan Talk About the Ku Klux Klan." *Look* (May 3, 1966): 36-44.

Garrow, David. *Bearing the Cross*. New York: Quill, 1986.

Gillette, Paul, and Eugene Tillinger. *Inside Ku Klux Klan*. New York: Pyramid, 1965.

Greene, Melissa. *The Temple Bombing*. New York: Fawcett Columbine, 1996.

Haas, Ben. *KKK*. New York: Tower, 1963.

Horn, Stanley. *Invisible Empire*. New York: Haskell House, 1968.

House Committee on Un-American Activities. *The Present-Day Ku Klux Klan Movement*. Washington, DC: U.S. Government Printing Office, 1967.

, Kenneth. *The Ku Klux Klan in the City, 1815-1930.* New York: Elephant
    aperbacks, 1967.
Kennedy, Stetson. *The Klan Unmasked.* Boca Raton: Florida Atlantic University Press, 1989.
Martin, John. *The Deep South Says "Never."* New York: Ballantine, 1957.
May, Gary. *The Informant.* New Haven, CT: Yale University Press, 2005.
McMillen, Neil. *The Citizens' Council.* Urbana: University of Illinois Press, 1971.
McWhorter, Diane. *Carry Me Home.* New York: Simon & Schuster, 2001.
Mendelsohn, Jack. *The Martyrs.* New York: Harper & Row, 1966.
National Association for the Advancement of Colored People. *Thirty Years of Lynching in
    the United States, 1889-1919.* New York: Negro Universities Press, 1919.
Niven, David. *The Politics of Injustice.* Knoxville: University of Tennessee Press, 2003.
Nunnelley, William. *Bull Connor.* Tuscaloosa: University of Alabama Press, 1991.
O'Reilly, Kenneth. *"Racial Matters."* New York: Free Press, 1989.
Parker, Thomas (ed.). *Violence in the U.S., Volume 1, 1956-67.* New York: Facts on File, 1974.
Rice, Arnold. *The Ku Klux Klan in American Politics.* Washington, DC: Public Affairs Press,
    1962.
Rowe, Gary Jr. *My Undercover Years with the Ku Klux Klan.* New York: Bantam, 1976.
Sherrill, Robert. *Gothic Politics in the Deep South.* New York: Grossman, 1968.
Sims, Patsy, *The Klan.* New York: Stein and Day, 1978.
Stanton, Mary. *Freedom Walk.* Oxford: University Press of Mississippi, 2003.
—. *From Selma to Sorrow.* Athens: University of Georgia Press, 1998.
Trelease, Allen. *White Terror.* New York: Harper, 1971.
Van Der Veer, Virginia. "Hugo Black and the KKK." *American Heritage Magazine* (April
    1968): 108-11.
Velie, Lester. "The Klan Rides the South Again." *Collier's* (Oct. 9, 1948): 13-16, 74-6.
Wade, Wynn. *The Fiery Cross.* New York: Oxford University Press, 1987.